Endorsements

"We all feel discouraged in life at some point; maybe even defeated. Have you felt unimportant or forgotten by family or God? Ever felt forsaken? Jerry and Kate have been there, done that. Their story includes severe child abuse and kidnapping, divorce, an unjust legal process, abandonment, manipulative parents, and much more. And yet, through God's power, they've been restored. And you can be, too. Whatever your circumstances Forsaken will inspire you to hang on and invite you to deepen your faith in the Lord. Read it and share it with someone you love. You are not forsaken."

~ **Ron L. Deal**
Family Trainer, Therapist, and
Bestselling Author of *The Smart Stepfamily*

"Jerry and Kate Angelo are passionate marriage advocates. If you have ever thought, "No one understands what I'm going though in my marriage," read this book. Forsaken validates what many couples experience while giving each spouse hope. Jesus breathes life into dead marriages."

~ **Ted Cunningham**
Pastor at Woodland Hills Family Church
Author of *Fun Loving You*

"Jerry and Kate are a unique couple who are blessed with a great vision on how to strengthen marriages. Their creativity and dedication to grow a movement to honor marriages is inspiring to all. The story of their journey in this book will be sure to provide encouragement to anyone who reads it."

~ **Roger Gibson**
Marriage & Family Pastor at Fellowship of
the Parks Church and Founder of Man Up & Go

"This book is sure to encourage you as you read of a story of two lives coming from harsh backgrounds, blending together after divorces, walking through difficult court battles and yet determined to Glorify God through helping others in their marriages. Overcoming child abuse and an all-out legal attack, are just a couple of compelling parts to the Angelos' story. Yet they took the difficult trials in life, and with God's grace constantly deciding not to hold onto bitterness but instead be an example of mercy and love."

~ **Molly Godzich**
Founder and Executive Director of
National Association of Marriage Enhancement (NAME)

I am happy to recommend "Forsaken" by Jerry and Kate Angelo to the reader. For many years I have known this wonderful couple. Well, I thought I knew them. Then, I read "Forsaken" myself. After reading the first two chapters, I knew what was about to happen. So, I went into my garage, got my folding zero gravity chair and proceeded to my backyard under the tree where I do my best reading. I spent a most enjoyable afternoon going through the emotional ups and downs contained in the story of these amazing people and their family. I could not put the book down, and felt anticipation every time I came to the end of Jerry's story, wanting to hear Kate's version of what had happened. The unique dual author style keeps the reader's attention and allows him or her to enjoy looking at the daunting mountains and despairing valleys they faced together, as One. The book shows us how a strong marriage with Christ at the center is truly a TEAM effort. Time after time Team Angelo steps up to the plate and takes their cuts at the game of life. The message of this book is uplifting, faith building, and leaves the reader with the feeling of joy to be a child of our wonderful loving Father in heaven. Both thumbs up, high up, for this inspiring book!

~ **Van Benson**
President and Executive
Trainer of Motive Matters LLC

forsaken

a journey of faith and purpose

Jerry and Kate Angelo

FORSAKEN

Published by Marriage Awakening LLC in Springfield, MO
Copyright © 2016 by Jerry and Kate Angelo All Rights Reserved
Cover Photo Copyright © 2016 by Jerry and Kate Angelo All Rights Reserved
Cover Design and Artwork Copyright © 2016 by Jerry and Kate Angelo All Rights Reserved

No part of this book may be reproduced, copied, or transmitted in any form without written permission prior to intended use. The only exception allowed is brief excerpts for review purposes.

Although every precaution has been taken to verify the accuracy of the information contained herein, the author and publisher assume no responsibility for any errors or omissions. No liability is assumed for damages that may result from the use of information contained within.

All Scripture quotations, unless otherwise indicated, are taken from the Holy Bible, New International Version®, NIV®. Copyright ©1973, 1978, 1984, 2011 by Biblica, Inc.™ Used by permission of Zondervan. All rights reserved worldwide. www.zondervan.com The "NIV" and "New International Version" are trademarks registered in the United States Patent and Trademark Office by Biblica, Inc.™

Library of Congress Control Number: 2018904221
ISBN-13: 978-0-9974081-2-6
First Edition Reprinted 2018

http://marriageawakening.com

To God be the Glory

My God, my God, why have you forsaken me?

Table of Contents

Acknowledgements 11

Preface 15

A Boy's Life 21

A Girl's Life 39

Life's Trials 61

A Girl Called 71

Boy Meets Girl 89

Girl Marries Boy 99

More Trials 115

Finding Happily Ever After 127

Truth and Purpose 147

Receiving the Promise 165

Forsaken 177

Acknowledgements

I'd like to thank God for granting me the grace and wisdom to pursue this project, without Him I am nothing. There have been a lot of tears shed and heartaches that were re-lived, but I know it was all for a greater purpose.

My sweetheart, Kate, I love you and I adore you. Thank you for walking beside me all these years. God gives purpose to life, but you make my purpose fun and worth all the effort. Thank you for writing this book with me. I know this story will touch many lives.

To our kids, we are so thankful to be chosen as your parents. There is piece of you that will live in my heart forever. I know it hasn't always been easy, but I have always loved each and every one of you. I pray God's blessing on your lives that it will be fruitful and full of purpose.

To our family, we thank you for your prayers, love, and support. Our church families, there are so many of you to thank. We couldn't possibly put them all in here. Chances are that you made some impression upon our lives over the years, and for that we are thankful. Please know that we cherish the connections we have made with all our friends over the years.

Raymond and Cynthia Frizzelle, we are forever grateful to you both. In the early years of our ministry you believed in us and allowed us to begin our ministry roots in your church. Your encouragement through our times of trial will never be matched. Thank you for your prayer, friendship, and love all these years.

Darrell and Kathey Wyrick, we are very blessed to have your friendship. Thank you for helping us along our path in ministry. We cherish our times together, and we think of you often when we reminisce of our beginnings in marriage ministry.

Leo and Molly Godzich, your heart and passion for marriages to be saved for the Kingdom of Christ Jesus is amazing. You inspired us to go deeper and seek a bigger vision in our ministry. Thank you for your friendship and trusting us to come to the International Marriage Conference to speak and encourage couples in the Lord Jesus.

Ted and Robbin Cederblom, your friendship, affirmation, encouragement, and trust is an invaluable resource to us. We are so thankful to you for your willingness to help us build up the ministry through the years.

Tim and Melanie Cederblom, your family has been a great example and encouragement to our family. Thank you for your friendship and for always being there for all of us when we needed it.

Van and Tammy Benson, thank you for sharing your insight and wisdom with us. Your friendship has made a lasting impact on our hearts. It has been an honor to serve beside you in ministry. We look forward to many other opportunities that we will share together.

Roger Gibson, thank you so much for making time for me. I think back to our days of white-boarding ministry ideas in your office. It was fun dreaming of the day when we would be able to implement them. Thanks for being a good friend.

Ron Deal, meeting you at a speaking engagement was a divine appointment. Becoming friends was definitely the bonus. We are thankful that you invited us to be on a broadcast with you at FamilyLife Today so that we could share our message with couples in need.

Ted Cunningham, it was fun and unexpected meeting you. It was even better after we heard your heart for marriages. Thanks for being a friend and being willing to let us tag along so that we could learn the value of laughter in marriage. We look forward to more laughter with you on the comedy tour.

Eric Johnson, Chris Davis, and Tony Mareshie, we want to thank you for helping us find a way to fight for our children. Your sincerity and passion for standing behind us in our pursuit of the truth and justice did not go unnoticed. We are also grateful for your friendship.

Ziva Branstetter, thank you for your excellence in investigative journalism. We appreciate your courage to print the truth, and your effort to bring our story into the light.

We feel so very blessed to have been a part of Africa's Hope where we were spiritually mentored during the early years of our marriage. We thank each of you for your prayers, love, and guidance. Having prayer warriors like you in our camp made an amazing difference in our lives.

We would also like to thank our friends who were special contributors to this project. Cyndi Norman, thank you for helping us with the editing process. Peter and Vanessa Pyo, thank you for being our "body doubles" on our book cover while we took the photo.

Preface

About three in the afternoon Jesus cried out in a loud voice, "Eli, Eli, lema sabachthani?" (which means 'My God, my God, why have you forsaken me?')

~ Matthew 27:46

How could God, the one who promises never to leave us nor forsake us, turn His back on His only begotten Son, Jesus Christ? If God had forsaken His own Son during the most difficult point in Jesus' life, then how can we trust Him to keep His promise to us?

Is God trustworthy? Is this promise that is recorded in His Word, the Holy Bible, a contradiction? Or is God deceiving us by giving us false hope?

I wanted to trust God. I wanted to believe God and His promises. Yet, this Scripture passage really bothered me. My discomfort with this passage and the questions it created in me only seemed to continue throughout the years.

I couldn't even begin to predict how my discomfort and questioning would slowly become resolved as I began writing this book with my wife. One by one over the years my questions were being answered and even began to make sense the more God's Spirit revealed His perfect wisdom. The more I experienced God's unconditional love, the more I began to understand the lengths God's love would go for me and all mankind. Only then did I begin to appreciate the most amazing relationship ever known.

It didn't happen immediately. It took a journey that spanned several years, and many times it was filled with disappointment and heartache. Even then, this journey only provided some of the answers I was seeking.

This journey seems at times like a giant jigsaw puzzle. A puzzle that *requires* my participation. A puzzle that I must choose on a daily basis to follow someone else's directions. A puzzle that doesn't guarantee immediate completion.

Day by day and piece by piece I grew increasingly aware of the commitment I must make. Instinctively, I realize completion of this puzzle is a slow process, one that will take a lifetime before it will truly be complete. As with any puzzle, I didn't know where to begin. As I began to realize what was at stake and given the number of possibilities, I questioned if it was even possible to successfully complete the puzzle, let alone complete it correctly.

When I *first* began this journey, I was so sure I could handle this puzzle called life on my own. I was equally certain I would succeed. I remember feeling a rush of excitement as the pieces of my life seemed to fall into place. Pieces called independence, employment, education, marriage, and family. In the beginning, I chose pieces without ever seeking direction from anyone, let alone God. To my surprise, the pieces didn't fit very well.

The tricky part in this journey is realizing that God has a plan for me. We must trust that plan and the vision that He has given us. We must also receive the faith that He gives us to believe that His plan is a good plan and it will come to pass. A faith that knows His plan is designed specifically for me to successfully complete my journey, and for the pieces of my life to fit together flawlessly the way He intended.

The key to successfully completing my journey is simple, but it's not easy. It's simple because all I need is to trust God. It's not easy because I must put myself aside and trust God. I must choose to trust His plan for me. I must choose to trust His vision for me and the vision He placed inside me. I must choose to believe in someone that I can't see, a path that I don't know, and a calling that feels overwhelming. At the same time, remaining confident that what I hope for in this journey will actually happen. God calls it "faith."

This journey has been so incredible I decided to share my story. I asked my wife, Kate, to help me and to tell her story alongside mine. Because we wrote this book together from two distinctly different perspectives, it seemed logical to alternate each segment of our stories. By doing this, hopefully you, the reader, will gain a better perspective of our journey, our puzzle, and of God's amazing love for each of us.

We hope this book provides an opportunity to gain a glimpse of the multiple souls, their complexity, and how they all converge into one story of God's beautiful masterpiece. You will follow our journey and see a family experience their challenges and also their joy. We hope this book provides insight into the trials and the blessings that our daily choices produce.

Through our story, we hope to show that marriage and family are more complicated than anyone ever dreams. It is also far more rewarding and full of more purpose than anyone could ever imagine. We hope our story reveals some of the challenges and the joys that came about while we were blending our family together.

It is our sincere desire that this book will open the eyes and hearts of people who have felt devastation on their journey and those who find themselves questioning God. For those just beginning their journey, we hope this book will help provide some much needed direction.

More importantly, we hope that we can inspire you to learn to put your trust in Almighty God and your faith in His Son, Jesus Christ. He is the only one who can guide you safely through this journey called life. He is the only one who can truly help you, restore you, and heal you.

I pray this book provides hope and encouragement to you along your journey and in your moments of despair.

A Boy's Life

This is what the LORD says: "Cursed is the one who trusts in man, who draws strength from mere flesh and whose heart turns away from the LORD. That person will be like a bush in the wastelands; they will not see prosperity when it comes. They will dwell in the parched places of the desert, in a salt land where no one lives. But blessed is the one who trusts in the LORD, whose confidence is in him. They will be like a tree planted by the water that sends out its roots by the stream. It does not fear when heat comes; its leaves are always green. It has no worries in a year of drought and never fails to bear fruit."

~ Jeremiah 17:5-8

Many times when I meet someone new and I'm getting to know them I tell them, *"I come from a long line of east coast, Italian, Catholics".* They usually chuckle so then I follow it up with more truthful clichés, *"I even have relatives that I call Uncle Tony and also my cousin Vinny."*

All this would be said with the appropriate New York accent of course. Sometimes I even mention that I was an altar boy when I was younger just to complete the stereotype. This is funny to me now that my wife and I are both ministers with the Assembly of God. When I look back at my life now, silly situations like this help me realize that I wasn't always so willing to yield to God's calling or even take my faith as seriously as I should have.

If fact, I didn't really enjoy being an altar boy. Well, maybe at first I did so that I could please my parents. It did feel good to be honored and respected by other people in the congregation as they watched me perform the rituals that only I could do. The ringing of ceremonial bells, the handling the incense during the sacred prayers, I must admit it was pretty cool being that close to all the action, but every single Sunday – *come on, too much.*

Some things I can remember like it was yesterday. Like the quiet, ever so slight, calling of the Lord in my life. Several people would even come up to me and say, *"You should be a Sunday school teacher."*

Then there were those times when people would say to me, *"You should be a pastor someday."* I usually shrugged off those comments and thought that wasn't for me, probably for some selfish reason at the time. You see I didn't have time for that, I thought I had a better plan in mind.

It's not that I didn't believe in God, I did. Especially after all those years of church catechism classes and then those confirmation classes, I knew there was a God of the universe. I was proud of that fact, I even tried to *prove* that there was a God to several of my friends, many times although probably for the wrong reasons. I just didn't really know how to relate to Him in a very real and personal way.

I was born into a family with five children. I was the only boy surrounded by four sisters. My two oldest sisters are about nine and eleven years older than me. About seven years separates me from my third sister who was born right before me. Another seven years separates me from my youngest sister. Being the only boy and the large age gap between me and my siblings made it easy for me to pretend like I was an only child, except for that pesky younger sister who was always trying to get me in trouble.

Even though I grew up in a house where I was fortunate to have my own bedroom, it could feel really small at times. Living in an Italian family with my father, five women, and lots of extended family around could prove challenging at times. Especially when I needed to use the bathroom.

I learned very quickly the ways of being independent, at least as much as an aspiring teenager could on their own. As soon as I could, I began earning money. It was very empowering and gave me a sense of control in my life. I started out with odd jobs and mowing lawns to save money for my first Commodore 64 computer system. Remember those? I saved and traded up to a motorcycle and eventually my first car. Now that I had reliable transportation, I began to pursue more traditional ways of earning money like getting my first real job. I worked four days at a local fast food restaurant until I received a better offer at the local grocery store.

As I began to work my way through the ranks at each progressively more successful job opportunity, I also reaped the reward of success at a young age. Even when I made some seemingly bad choices from time to time, things always seemed to turn around quickly for me. I enjoyed the many fruits of my labor, and as the jobs got better, the money got better. I attributed God's favor in my life to be the fruit of my own ambition. I was thankful to God for what He had provided me, but many times it was an afterthought.

Growing up at home for me was pretty good, not perfect, but good. My dad was the sole income earner, and my mom was a stay-at-home mom and homemaker. I may not have had the best of everything, but I never lacked anything. Even though we had our ups and downs, my parents did a good job taking care of us.

We were a close-knit family. We still are. The years seemed to fade our closeness when my sisters and I grew up and moved away to attend college or get married. But the close bond we shared growing up was not only rekindled, it is strengthened whenever we all get together again for holidays and special events.

It was a weekly tradition for us to come together for a family meal. Every Sunday after church my extended family and my grandparents would always go out for lunch together, and my grandparents would always insist on paying. Even as a teenager, I made a point to go with them because as kids were taught the importance of family and tradition. The free meal was a nice bonus.

After a while, I began to share my sisters' desire for independence. As they got older, they began planning what they were going to do once they were old enough to leave the home. I also had an increased longing to be out on my own. I enjoyed the independence of doing my own thing although I secretly desired to be known and loved.

As I was growing up I learned some tough lessons at a young age. Some of these lessons even continued through my teen years, and eventually as an adult. It was that people could not be trusted. You see, I held a high value on loyalty, and the only way I could trust you is if I noticed that you were loyal. This took time. It wasn't easy to come into my "circle of trust". Occasionally I would make an exception and invite some of my closest friends in.

Over the years I did let people into that "circle of trust" in my heart. Many of them were trustworthy and loyal, but some of them were not, although they appeared to be. I let myself be vulnerable to those people. I poured my heart out into those trusted relationships. These were people I loved and trusted dearly.

Over time, one by one some of them let me down. Some of them betrayed me and let me down in a big ways. This began a hardening process in my heart. I began to be very cautious and skeptical about people getting too close to me. I was constantly guarding and protecting myself from others.

Little did I know that this was exactly the opposite of what I was longing for. These repeated disappointments only reinforced my view of self-preservation. This also reminded me that ultimately I could not trust anyone. The problem with not trusting anyone is that you can't get close to them either. This desire I had to be known and loved meant that I must also risk my heart. I wasn't sure what to do about this, and it troubled me.

After high school I took a couple of years off to work, but later I decided that I wanted to go to college. Some friends of mine suggested that I join a fraternity, and the next thing I knew I was "in." It wasn't a very godly environment, but I did learn a few things about respect and honor. I made several lifelong friends who I even keep in contact with to this day.

I was having fun in college, but I wanted more. I was ready to be close to someone again. I met someone and things went fast at first. The next thing I knew we were in a relationship. We dated for quite a while, and about 2 years later we were married. A few years after that, it was as if I blinked and we had 2 wonderful and beautiful children. I didn't expect how this would change me. Things were a little different now. I loved being a dad in every way, but this was also a big responsibility and I was cautiously excited by this honor.

I really enjoyed work and continued building my career. Once again I received favor with promotions and salary with a great employer. It was the perfect job for someone in my line of work, and the projects I was put in charge of only increased my success. At the time I also thought I was bringing success to my home. That's what the world tells you to do. Work hard to provide for your family...*right*?

With each project I was given, it was completed not only on-time, but early and under budget. This boosted my confidence and my ambition grew with each success. More money, more things, more comfortable lifestyle; this is what I was supposed to do along with doing what pleased me as well. I was making a better life for me and for my family. At the time, I didn't realize that I was being blinded by all the distractions. I really thought I was doing my duty as a husband and father.

All of the sudden the bottom started to fall out...of everything. You see, I was beginning to believe that there wasn't anything I couldn't do on my own. I had started from nothing, and through years of hard work I actually had something. I had something great, but I thought it was all due to my accomplishments. God was an afterthought...*thanks dude for the stuff*. That was my attitude. I thanked him so disingenuously. Oh, I cried out to Him with my whole heart when I needed something, but He wasn't done working in my life. He was only just beginning.

Things continued to decline for me and my family. It was like two steps forward three steps backward. The company I was working for filed for

Chapter 11 and I was eventually laid off. I became a casualty of the technology bubble that burst in the early 2000's. At first it wasn't bad because I was actually able to begin my own company doing what I loved. I enjoyed initial success, but things went downhill rapidly after that. Our marriage was experiencing serious problems. This is when I knew I couldn't do this on my own, and I finally realized that I needed God.

I didn't have time for my customers anymore, and the business started failing because I was doing everything I could to work on the marriage. There was plenty of blame to go around in our relationship, but I thought we could overcome the challenges we faced. I put everything I had into saving the situation, but it was too late...she left.

Up to this point, this was the most devastating thing to happen in my life. Another betrayal. How could I ever trust someone again? The pain was so deep and penetrating I almost couldn't bear it.

I did the only thing I could do and that was cry out to God. Slowly but surely as my cries softened I began to hear His voice inside my heart. You see, some weeks before the divorce I humbled myself before the Lord. I wholeheartedly submitted to Him only after I prayed the sinner's prayer in the pastor's office of a tiny little AG church. I asked Jesus Christ into my heart to live forever.

In that moment He showed me that one of the mistakes I was making is that I kept putting people in His place. This was something I learned in deception from the world. I quickly realized that this must stop.

All those years I put the ones I loved, one-by-one, on a high pedestal in my heart where only God should have been. When each one of them failed me I was devastated, and my world came crashing down. He wasn't saying I shouldn't let them into my heart, just not in God's place. That way I could experience His love that would never fail me even in my disappointment. From that moment, things slowly began to turn around. It was a large ship to turn, but I was making progress.

Like I said earlier through all my Catholic instruction and upbringing, I knew who God was, but I didn't necessarily *know* Him. At least I thought I knew who He was. I started to realize there was so much more to know and best of all I could know Him personally. I started to reach out for Him everywhere I could. I went to several churches looking for help. Some of them didn't know what to do with me. Some offered kindness, and one nice lady even gave me an audio taped series of Gary Chapman's, *"Five Love Languages."* I graciously accepted the gift although I had heard it a few weeks earlier. I was just hoping it would have been on CD, who uses cassette tapes anymore.

I was spiritually wandering from place to place when I came upon another truly caring soul. She was actually one of my former customers. She invited me to her new church gathering that was meeting in the sanctuary of another church while they were trying to get established. This was quite a development because I was breaking 30 years of tradition and not attending a Catholic church. I didn't even know what denomination they were, but I knew this little band of believers loved God and it was real.

I had many prayers back then and one of them was that I wanted His wisdom and direction for my life. The church members began to sing and worshipped with such passion; it was amazing to me. When they sang the song, *"Open the Eyes of My Heart"* it grabbed my attention immediately. I had never heard this song before, but instantly it was as if my spirit was talking directly to God about my request.

All those years of religious instruction and knowledge, and I had never felt the presence of God like that until now. I wanted more. After the service ended, they invited me to their morning bible study and I readily accepted.

Once again I wouldn't normally attend a bible study so early in the morning out of the blue like that, but I was hungry to learn more about the journey I was on with the Lord. There was also the fact that I had previously taken a job delivering newspapers to help make ends meet and I had to get up at the crack of dawn anyway. So, there was a good chance I was going to make it to their next meeting.

As I read the bible more and more, I began to relate with the characters in it. I could see their pain and struggle to do right and overcome. Sometimes God favored them, but many times they were persecuted. The first character I really identified with was Job.

Although I wasn't blameless before the eyes of God, I did relate to his loss. He lost all he had in this world, and God allowed it to happen. That sure sounded a lot like me. Of course I left the part out where I *just really* started living for Christ and I wanted Him to get on my requests pronto. It gave me hope to know that even though I had consequences to face, I believed that eventually He would restore me just like He did for Job. That night I cried out for his mercy to restore me once again.

The next day I was up early delivering newspapers and listening to the only luxury I had at the time. I had one of those satellite radio systems in my vehicle and it was pre-paid for several months. Listening to the Christian Talk Radio station became a regular habit, and I loved the teachings of several of the preachers on the radio. After my paper run was complete I stopped into the church where they were meeting that morning.

"So, you are the one I was praying for last night!" said the gentleman who met me as I was walking inside. When he said that I immediately had a puzzled look on my face, like what are you talking about? He must have seen the surprised look on my face as he continued, *"I woke up in the middle of the night and God prompted me to get down on my knees and begin praying for someone. Those prayers must have been for you!"*

I was shocked, how did he know I was crying out to God the night before? Maybe God heard me, but did He really cause this man to wake up and pray for me? Without being asked, everyone gathered around to lay hands on me and pray. I began to cry and prayed along with them. I felt the presence of God in our midst and felt a great peace among us.

Afterward, there was an elderly lady present who was there for the whole ordeal who came up to me. She was so bold and she said to me, *"I don't know what you did son, but if you ever want things to be right again you are going to have to do some things."*

She stopped talking for a moment as if she was waiting for me to write down what she was saying. I kind of chuckled inside and began to take notes. I don't know what she thought I had done, but she was serious about me taking down her advice. I wrote down everything she said. For months I had those notes, and I even carried them with me everywhere I went.

If fact, that is when I began journaling every day. I wrote down all kinds of things that inspired me and gave me encouragement or direction. Once I had that true change of heart to want to do things God's way instead of my own, so many people came up to me out of the blue to encourage me.

People I didn't know were speaking blessings into my life and imparting scriptures upon me that even remind me to this day of what God was doing in my life. I remember one day God used someone to say to me, that *"God will restore to me the years that the locust had eaten."* This was such an encouragement that I will remember for the rest of my life.

God used these moments to speak to my heart in such a way as to show me that if I repented of my sin, He would restore what had been stolen from me. I wouldn't avoid the consequences of any sin, but I knew that God would bring restoration to me and my family. I truly believe that God used those wonderful people to speak into my life and help guide me on my journey in the right direction to accomplish God's will in my life.

I found a great church and began attending regularly. I was hungry to really know God, and I was learning so much about Him. At the time I was devastated financially and there were several issues arising from the divorce. Even in those struggles, He continued to be so good to me despite some of the challenges I was going through.

After being laid off from probably one of the best technical jobs in the region, taking the huge severance package I was given to start a business, and then seeing that business fail when I tried to save the marriage. To say I was struggling in more ways than one was an understatement.

I was also getting to the last two hundred dollars that I had in the whole world, and it was not enough to cover the upcoming rent or food for myself and two children. How could I have fallen so far financially? I had never *really* worried about money before, but this was scary.

I wanted God to be present in all areas in my life, and I was learning how to tithe at the time. I decided to give that a shot, why not? I gave the church twenty dollars, a tithe on all I had in the world. I had heard that God loves a cheerful giver, so I seriously had a smile on my face when I put the money in the offering. I literally laughed out loud! I wasn't going to take a chance and waste that money if I didn't believe in what I was doing.

A few days later I went to get the mail, and I was surprised to notice that there was a check in there. I couldn't believe it at first! It was a refund check for an insurance policy that I cancelled for the business. This was definitely unexpected.

A short time later, my phone rang. It was the church and they said they wanted me to come down there because they had something for me. I went down there and to my surprise they had written me a check for my rent that I couldn't pay on my own. I didn't think I told anyone about that, but God knew I needed it.

Just like that, I had all the provision I needed. It got even better. I landed an IT contract to go to work for a major oil company. It was a ninety minute commute to work each way, but they were going to pay me very well for my time.

For months I continued to get up early to get ready for this new job and to get the kids ready for daycare as well. I rushed off to work every day just to get there in the nick of time. Then I rushed back home again to pick up the kids, and finally I collapsed at home, all to begin again the very next day. Our needs were getting met and then some, but this was exhausting.

When I look back that that time now, that ninety minute drive each way actually began to be some of my favorite time of the day, after time with my kids of course. During that commuting time I listened to various preaching. This was a habit that I started several months earlier after purchasing the satellite radio system. This morning routine actually created an environment for me to focus and learn more about my increasing faith in Christ. God was actually using satellite technology to plant seeds into my heart.

I began to realize that I couldn't continue this exhausting daily routine forever. Then one day out of the blue I received a call for another great job opportunity. The only issue was that I had to relocate from Oklahoma to Missouri. I agonized over the thought of making a decision on this for days. I knew that this was going to force an issue that I would have to face with my children and their mother.

After much prayer and deliberation, I knew this was what God wanted me to do. I also knew the impossible challenges I would face as a result of this choice to pursue what God was calling me to do. The difference is, this choice I was making was His will for my life. No matter how well-meaning my previous choices were, I was tired of reaping the consequences of those self-directed decisions. In my pitiful defense, by society's standards I could say that I was always meeting my needs and the needs of my family. On the outside things didn't look so horrible, but these choices always seemed to result in an emptiness without real purpose.

Ultimately, I got honest with myself, and I analyzed the choices I made in the past. I realized that they always contained some element of a self-centered priority, and now it was time for a real shift in motivation. This was going to be something new and I believed that this opportunity was from God. It wasn't just what I thought was right, it is what God knew was right for me and my family. In the end, I decided to accept the job and began plans to relocate.

A Girl's Life

If you belonged to the world, it would love you as its own. As it is, you do not belong to the world, but I have chosen you out of the world. That is why the world hates you.

~ John 15:19

The world hates you. That sounded about right. Looking back at my childhood, it was easy to believe the world and everyone in it hated me. It was even easier to believe that God hated me as well. I grew up feeling like I could never do anything right. Given the circumstances throughout my childhood, I came to believe that I would never have a "normal" life.

The problem was, I had no idea what "normal" meant. I just knew that I wanted a different life. My entire childhood was full of chaos, leaving me to carry an enormous amount of baggage.

I recall my birth parents actually being together only a short time. During that time, I lived with them and two siblings in an old school bus that my parents had converted into a makeshift home. There were five of us in that rusty old bus. My parents had a bed at the back, and my father built a triple bunk for the children using two by fours and plywood.

Our family of five became a family of six when my parents brought a new baby brother home. I can still remember them placing him in a cardboard box at the end of their bed. We were all crammed into that old school bus living with no electricity and no running water.

Shortly after the birth of my youngest brother, my parents split up. Their relationship was always volatile – full of terrible arguments and fighting. However, when they split their fighting became so much worse. As a small child I didn't always understand what was going on, but somehow I thought they were fighting about me and my siblings. Little did I know they would fight bitterly for years over who would get custody of two of the children.

As a child, the difficult thing to understand was why my parents only fought over my older sister and me. I always knew that my older brother was my half-brother. It was no secret that my mother gave birth to him when she was only fifteen years old. I later learned that my father believed my new baby brother was the result of an affair. It was this which led to my parent's explosive separation. My mother denied the affair, but when it came to custody my father only wanted what he claimed were his - my sister and me.

My parents fought over me and my sister from the time I was very small until I was about ten or eleven years old. They would argue about us in front of us, followed by giving each other the silent treatment for long periods of time. This made us feel uncomfortable and confused. It didn't matter if they argued openly or silently, the atmosphere was toxic.

But, they didn't stop there. I remember both of my parents trying to "brainwash" us into believing the other parent was a terrible person. Even worse, my parents did something that proved to be far more devastating to us. They kidnapped us – again and again and again.

Anytime a child is kidnapped the perpetrator creates a trauma so catastrophic the child never fully recovers from its devastation. For the rest of their life that child will struggle constantly to escape its aftermath as they seek to become an independent person. This was also true for my sister and me.

Each time one parent would kidnap us, my sister and I were deeply traumatized. Our trauma wasn't just about the things we were forced to leave behind, such as clothes, favorite toys, and friends. Our trauma came about because we lived in constant fear and instability every single day of our life.

Both parents took turns stealing us whenever any opportunity presented itself. If they knew where we went to school, they would come there and take us. Before long, my sister and I learned to fear the loud beep just before an announcement came over the intercom. We knew that beep was often followed by a call for us to go to the office. When we got there, we would find one of our parents there to kidnap us.

Besides school, we began to fear the time between exiting the school door and getting onto the school bus. On any given day, we came to expect one of our parents to drive up and force us into their car. Even going to the grocery store to shop became extremely stressful for my sister and me. We never knew when we might run into our other parent who would roughly remove us from the grocery cart while no one was watching.

Each time we were taken we lost any sense of stability and safety. Time after time, we were thrown into abusive situations we couldn't control, with people we sometimes did not know.

My father worked toward becoming a truck driver in order to earn a decent living. While he trained for his new job, he worked during the day and went to school at night. During this period, he frequently left us with his mother, our grandmother. Unfortunately, it wasn't long before she became mentally unstable and took her own life.

Before she committed suicide, she tried to contact my mother to come and get us. My mother thought this was a trap, some ruse to get her arrested for the many outstanding warrants she had for check kiting. Out of fear, she never responded to my grandmother's pleas to come and get us, and she left us there.

One evening my grandmother tucked us into bed and kissed us good night just like we were used to. She made up her bed on the couch in the living room where she often slept. She smoked a cigarette, and before the cigarette was finished, she used a revolver to take her own life.

When we woke the next day, my sister and I tried to wake our grandmother from her deep sleep. Her bed sheets were often covered in cigarette burns from the many times she would pass out drunk while smoking. We couldn't have been much older than five and six years old, so it was natural that we didn't understand why she was sleeping so deeply that we couldn't wake her. We had often helped clean up the spilled drinks, tipped ashtrays, and sometimes the vomit from her drinking. On this day, I remember my sister trying to clean up the mess my grandmother had made when she "fell asleep".

Some days later, the police came and found that we had been with my grandmother for several days without anyone knowing what had happened. I believe that we were taken into custody by the Department of Family Services, and later returned to my father.

After my grandmother's death, my father finished his training and began working full time as a truck driver. With my grandmother gone, my father chose to leave us home alone, rather than find childcare. There were times when he left my sister and me home alone for days, and even weeks at a time. In between runs, he would come home, but only for a few days. We were barely school age.

When I was about seven years old, my father began dating a woman well over fifty years old. She had a daughter living with her who was close to my father's age. It wasn't long after they started dating that my father left my sister and me in the care of his new girlfriend and her daughter.

My sister and I never understood why he chose to date the mother rather than her daughter. The daughter seemed much younger, but then, there were a lot of things we didn't understand.

These two women abused my sister and me severely. We were physically tortured nearly every waking moment that my father was absent. It was seemingly for no reason other than pure hatred.

We were hit with wire coat hangers and burned with scalding water. They would beat us with belts, swinging the metal belt buckle wildly, sometimes catching us in the back, legs, arms, or face. We were forced to drink hot sauce, or stagnant water from the dog bowl outside. They choked us with their bare hands or with an electrical cord while screaming obscenities at us.

We were often locked in a closet and they denied us food and water. Other times, they chained us to a tree outside for hours in the hot Texas sun. They held us under water in the bathtub until we almost drowned. Many times they drug us around the house by our hair all while yelling and cursing at us over something we had done.

When they were extremely enraged, they would bite us so hard they ripped chunks of flesh from our bodies. At other times, they would scratch us so hard with their fingernails it looked like we'd been attacked by a lion.

My dad's extended absences allowed his girlfriend and her daughter to abuse us until a few days before his return home. My sister and I assumed this was to give our wounds a few days to heal and prevent my father from seeing physical signs of abuse. During those few days, they continued to burn us with cigarettes. Later, they simply claimed the burn marks were just mosquito bites we had scratched into sores.

My father failed to notice what was going on with us. The few times we attempted to tell him about the abuse, he refused to believe us. There was one, maybe two times, when he did confront them over something they had done to us. But, the women quickly convinced him anything we might have said was so outrageous we had to be lying. He chose to believe them.

After these efforts failed, the women escalated the severity of their abuse to torture so intense we never again considered or attempted to report them to anyone. Repeatedly, they beat us so severely we could do nothing, but lay broken, bruised, and bleeding.

My sister and I never understood why they treated us so badly. But then, how can any child understand why someone who was supposed to protect and nurture them chose instead to hurt them in such heinous ways?

Between living with my mother and my dad, I soon learned to take care of myself from a very early age. I don't remember exactly when this began, but I do recall being four or five years old when I did the shopping, the household chores, and even made sure we had food to eat.

In fact, I remember one time when I crossed Interstate Highway 10 in Houston, Texas, by myself. I was only six or seven years old, but I needed to get to the grocery store to buy a few packages of Raman Noodles so we'd have something to eat. Clearly, I was way too young to be left at home alone, let alone left to handle so many adult responsibilities on my own.

As bad as it had been living with my father, there was little safety for me when I went to live with my mother. While living with my mother, we had to deal with her boyfriends or husbands hitting us in anger. They would use their hands or their belts to beat us. However, nothing they did was as severe as those times spent in my father's care.

My mom never physically abused her children. But, the emotional abuse she dished out was, in many ways, far more devastating than any physical abuse.

My mother was an alcoholic. She drank from the time she woke up that day until she passed out that evening. As a result, she was completely unable to care for herself or anyone else, leaving us, her children, to fend for ourselves.

When she was sober, rather than spend what little money she had on food or clothing for her children, she chose, instead, to spend it on exotic animals. Her plan was to raise exotic animals and sell them at a profit. Unfortunately, her drinking made her unable to care for the animals.

While I did enjoy having a pet monkey, several exotic birds, multiple dogs, a baby bobcat, a ground hog, and even a lion cub, I was left with the responsibility to care for all of the animals. Imagine a ten-year-old girl trying to feed raw chicken to the pet lion my mother kept in our bathroom!

My older brother and sister began taking advantage of my mother's parenting or, lack thereof. Rather than rise and help care for their younger siblings or help with the chores around the house, they both did whatever they wanted. In the process, they left everything to me, including the care of my mother.

Before long, my older brother and sister were absent for extended periods of time. They were either running away from home, or in jail. Anytime they were home, they stayed only long enough to cause trouble. My brother was always getting into fights, drinking, and using drugs. Eventually, he got involved in religious cults that worshipped demons and made animal sacrifices. Later, he would turn away from this lifestyle and give his life to Jesus. But, he never did leave drugs and alcohol alone.

As a result, the police became a regular presence at our house. They came to break up fights between my brother and our step-father. Other times they came to break up fights between my mother and our step-father. Sometimes, they came to arrest my mother for passing bad checks. Whatever the reason, I soon came to fear the police. From this young child's perspective, they only came to a house to take someone to jail.

It didn't take long before my brother introduced my older sister to his lifestyle, addictions and all. Following his lead, she, too, became a slave to drug and alcohol addictions.

With my parents' permission, she got married at 15 years old. She was too young to be a wife, and I don't think she ever really knew what being a wife meant. All she wanted was a way to escape the craziness at home.

Soon after the wedding, she moved away. When she left, I felt she had abandoned me to take care of our mother and siblings. We had been through a lot together, and suddenly I was left alone. But she couldn't escape her habits, and eventually, she became a prostitute living and working for her next fix.

Sadly, both my brother and my sister died young. My brother died in his twenties from a drug overdose. My sister died in her early thirties from a disease she contracted from using a dirty needle.

When my parents finally gave up kidnapping my sister and me, I was around eleven years old. We were left with my mother and my father abandoned us completely. By that time, my mother had six children, adding two more sisters to the crew.

Even though my step-father didn't drink as much as my mother, he did spend most of his time and money smoking marijuana. Looking back, I think he did the best he knew how when it came to living with my mom and trying to raise us kids. For one thing, he saw how hard I worked to take care of my mother and siblings. He was concerned I was growing up way too fast.

Still, I remember being around twelve years old when he started waking me up early on Saturday and Sunday mornings. He would take me out and teach me how to drive our car. My mother had a bad habit of driving drunk, so he decided if we could convince her to let me drive when she had too much to drink it would be better for all of us. As it turns out, a sober twelve year old can drive a car better than an inebriated adult.

My step-father was growing increasingly more concerned for the well-being of me and my three younger siblings. He was concerned we were headed for the same trouble as my older brother and sister. Searching for a way to change our environment, he decided that a move out of Texas to another state might be a chance to start over.

When he found work in Springfield, Missouri, we packed up and moved. He rented a house in the country outside a small town north of Springfield. Moving from a big city to a small town and living in the country was quite a culture shock for me. Yet, I found myself excited. I began to hope for the first time that we really could have a different life.

Compared to what I had experienced so far, this really was a new life. I entered high school as a freshman and a whole new world opened up to me. This new world included new friends, a new school, a new culture, and a lot of new experiences. Coming from a big city in Texas, I felt like a city mouse amidst a lot of country mice.

Even so, it really was a great new start. I quickly made new friends. People were attracted to my Texas accent and frequent use of the word "y'all." If that didn't impress them, then watching my reaction to seeing snow for the first time did. In fact, everything seemed to set me apart.

There were so many adjustments to make in this new, but small town life. Unlike city life, there were no gangs to cause concern. In fact, there didn't seem to be any crime at all. Unlike my previous school, the kids in my new school didn't appear to be buying and selling sex or drugs. Instead, they spent their time "cruisin' the strip" or rushing home in time to milk the cows before dinner.

Yet, despite the new start, life at home didn't change all that much. My step-father still worked long hours. Our new house meant he had a long commute, which only increased his absence at home. My mother continued to buy and sell exotic animals, which continued to cause a financial strain on the family and added more responsibilities on me.

While she did slow down on her drinking, she never stopped completely. Her drinking continued to leave the burden of care for the house, the kids, the animals, and even her, on me. When she drank too much, it would be me who helped her into bed. I was the one who made sure the little ones had their baths and did their homework. Even though I was now only thirteen, I continued to drive mom around when she had too much to drink.

Because my step-father saw I was growing into a capable young woman he encouraged me to get a job. He thought I should begin earning money so I could create a better life for myself. I started out by helping him do side jobs during the summer.

Eventually, I got a job working at a fast food restaurant in town. The manager never knew how young I was, and thankfully he never checked. This meant that I was able to work as many hours as I wanted or needed.

Almost a year after we moved to Missouri, my step-father decided to leave my mother. My mother and I came home after spending a long day out of town only to find all of his things were gone. Even worse, he took my two and a half year old sister with him. He gave no notice and left no note. He just disappeared into thin air. I had no idea that when I left that morning to run errands with my mom, it would be the last time I would ever see either of them again.

In response, my mother decided to search for her daughter by returning to Texas. She was, after all, an expert on finding and kidnapping her children. She left me in charge of my younger brother and sister. She left us with twenty dollars, some food stamps and a promise. She promised she would return in a few days with our sister. But days turned into weeks, and weeks turned into months yet we never heard a word from her.

I worried about my mother, but mostly I worried about me. How was I to continue going to school and work while taking care of two children? How could I pay the bills or buy groceries for the three of us? What would I do if my mother never returned? I felt abandoned and scared.

It wasn't long before my teachers began to chide me for not completing my homework or being late to school. They had no idea what I was going through at home, nor did they ask. They didn't know I was a teenager living the life of an adult, completely ill-equipped to handle my circumstances, and completely lacking in financial support.

My responsibilities included getting my siblings up each morning, getting them dressed, and feeding them breakfast before leaving for school. I would go directly from school to work most days. If I could, I would work until after eleven every night.

I desperately needed the money, so I worked as many hours as I possibly could. I felt bad that my brother and sister were now the ones left alone while I worked. But, I didn't know what else to do.

The routine was really beginning to take its toll on me. I was exhausted physically, emotionally, and mentally.

Eventually, our teachers began to notice something wasn't quite right. We barely had enough money for food, much less clothes or toiletries. Eventually, a child protection worker came to our house to investigate.

My mother finally returned home, but only after my brother and sister were taken away by the police and placed in a foster home. I felt so guilty. I felt responsible for failing to keep us together while my mother was gone.

A caseworker explained to me that it wasn't my fault for what happened to my siblings. For the first time in my life, someone told me it wasn't my job to be the parent. I had no idea. I had never *not* been a parent. I had no idea how to be anything else.

The caseworker explained that the reason I was allowed to stay in my home was because I was old enough to be left alone while my mom was away for short periods of time. My siblings, on the other hand, were not. They were too young to be left alone, so they needed to be placed in a safe home.

She tried to encourage me by saying they would return home as soon as my mother could prove she was able to properly provide for them. My mother also needed to prove she could provide them with a safe home, proper food to eat, and all the necessities they needed.

She also told me that if I felt my living situation was not safe, I, too, could go into foster care while my mom pulled herself together. At first, this sounded absurd to me. Why would I ever go into a foster home and leave my mom alone? In my heart I knew she couldn't do what they were asking of her, because she could barely take care of herself.

Because of her drinking, her inability to manage money, and her stress over losing her marriage and her daughter, I was convinced she needed me. Without me there, I was afraid she would give up and drink herself to death. But most of all, I was afraid her inability to cope would be my fault.

Yet, I was tired. So very tired. Tired of being the adult. So very tired of always missing out on all the things other kids my age enjoyed; things like high school social activities, dances, and football games. Up to now,

I had never been able to participate in sports, school clubs, or even attend school events.

I was tired of missing out on what remained of my childhood. For as long as I could remember, there had never been any time for me to do anything but take care of family. No one had ever taken care of me.

I lived a life filled with abuse, neglect, abandonment, and completely forgotten by those around me. Now someone was offering me a chance at a different life – a life where at least one person in this world promised to care about me.

So, in front of a judge, my case worker, several attorneys, and my mother, I told the court I wanted to go into foster care. I will never forget the look on my mother's face. I could have plunged a dagger into her heart and she wouldn't have looked more hurt. It was probably the first time in her life that she realized her actions had caused so much pain and misery for her children.

Following the court hearing, my caseworker sent me to a different foster home than my siblings. She wanted to protect me from reverting back to parenting them. I was allowed to visit them only a few times, but the goal was to help me recover and to feel free to be a child.

My new home was so different from anything I had ever known. For one thing, it included rules and schedules. Plus, there was someone to take care of me, rather than me take care of them. It took time, but I started to feel safe in this new home. At the same time, I felt useless.

My role as a parent had been taken from me. I no longer knew who I was or what I was expected to do. My foster parents were great to me, but I was really struggling with my identity.

Shortly after I went into foster care, some of the girls at school invited me to attend their Wednesday night church group. I thought this was probably because the small town rumor mill had been informed of what had happened. I didn't want their pity.

At first, I made up excuses about not having time to go to church. In reality, I finally did have time for church, but I didn't want to waste it on God.

After all, God had abandoned me to a life filled with torture and pain. He never rescued me from child abuse. He never gave me parents who loved and cared for me. He forced me to choose between myself or my mother, foster care or a horrible life.

How could I bring myself to consider, let alone serve a God who had done all that to me? From my perspective, God had really forsaken me.

Life's Trials

For I know the plans I have for you," declares the LORD, "plans to prosper you and not to harm you, plans to give you hope and a future."

~ *Jeremiah 29:11*

My new company had relocated me and the children to Missouri. Things were really looking up for us. My new job was really great. It was flexible and family friendly. After some searching, we found a great church and began to make some new friends. God was continuing to restore me as He had promised.

At my first day on the job a major network technology company took my team to lunch. This was standard practice for the local representative to treat their customers to lunch in order to discuss any issues we may have with equipment, as well as inform us of any upcoming technology they might try to sell to us.

That day one of their system engineers mentioned to me that he was leaving their company. They had also brought in his replacement for us to meet over lunch. When I inquired as to the reasons for his departure, he said that he was going into the ministry to pursue God's calling on his life. This was a company that I had always dreamed of joining someday, as I'm sure many people in that line of work would dream of joining as well. Of all the days for me to go to lunch with these folks, of all the days for this person to leave their company, of all the reasons for that person to leave such a successful career, this moment truly stood out in my mind.

As the months flew by I continued to recall that moment at lunch. I admired his courage to step out in faith in such a bold venture for the Kingdom of Heaven. I secretly hoped for my opportunity to serve in a large ministry someday. I continued to seek the Lord daily, and I could feel that God was preparing me for something. He was affecting my heart in a tremendous way.

A series of significant moments happened one week when my job sent me to Dallas, TX for some special network training. The joint custody arrangement of the children at the time was, one full week for me with the children, then their mother would have her opportunity for one full week. I was ending my week, and I decided to drop the children off with their mother in Oklahoma while I was on my way to training.

Throughout the divorce and relocation we had all been through a lot, and God was teaching me not to be bitter. I still had a lot of pain, resentment, and feelings of betrayal that I was sorting through, but I was learning how to truly forgive.

One day I heard some scriptures that hit me like a brick. In verse 14 and 15 of Matthew 6 which comes directly after the Lord's prayer is this passage, *"For if you forgive other people when they sin against you, your heavenly Father will also forgive you. But if you do not forgive others their sins, your Father will not forgive your sins."*

That is some pretty tough medicine to swallow after going through the ordeal I just went through. I may have had plenty of reasons to be angry and not forgive, but I did not have a right to withhold forgiveness of others, especially if I wanted to participate in the forgiveness of my own sins. I was bought with a price. I thought to myself *no one is worth missing Heaven over,* and I decided right then that I would be obedient to God and learn to forgive those who wronged me.

This was quite a departure from my behavior in the past. I always kept a record in my mind of those who wronged me and I was sure not to forget it. This decision to forgive others was surely going to stretch me in ways that I had not been stretched before. At the time I didn't realize how valuable a lesson this was going to be in my life, but I was quickly coming upon my first real test.

When I arrived to return the children to their mother's house I was full of emotions about how I was feeling and what I was about to do. Even though our divorce had been finalized several months before, I wanted there to be peace between our two households. Even though I struggled with thinking that I was the one who had been wronged, I was planning on asking her to forgive me for my part with the hope that I would be able to forgive her as well.

I felt God calling me to be the one to go first, but this was not going to be easy. I prepared myself in prayer before approaching the door. When I dropped the kids off, I hugged and kissed them. As they headed inside I told them that I would miss them, but I would also see them soon. Before closing the door I asked their mother if I could speak to her for a moment and she obliged.

I knew what I had to say, must be said. I don't remember the exact words, but I basically asked her to forgive me for my part in all of the mess that we created. Wait a minute. What was I doing? Why did I ask that of her? In my mind I tried to rationalize that she should be asking *my* forgiveness, not the other way around, but I knew this was the right thing to do. Her response...not a word. Seriously, nothing. I waited for a moment then turned to leave.

That was OK. This was something that I needed to do and it wasn't conditional upon a response. What I realized was that forgiveness wasn't really for the person who has wronged you. It was part of a process by which you release another person from the hurt they have inflicted upon you. In that moment, along with asking her to forgive me, I also forgave her for all that she had done to me. I don't know if she ever forgave me, but I knew in that moment I was released from the huge weight of unforgiveness that I had previously been carrying around with me.

This one act of obedience to God caused a shift in my way of thinking. It forever changed my heart. In some strange way when I humbled myself like I did, it mysteriously unlocked a potential that gave me the understanding for how to truly forgive someone. A smile in my heart slowly began to form...this was definitely something God was going to continue to test me with.

On the six hour drive to the training facility in Dallas, TX I felt a great peace come over me, and I knew that God was doing something new in me. He spoke to my heart and gave me the sense that he was setting me apart for something special. I didn't know what that was, but only that I need to trust Him and obey His commands. I wanted to please Him like every son wants to please His father, so my heart was open to His message for me.

    I arrived at my hotel that night and it was late. It was a clear night and very warm outside. I decided to take a swim and relax before bed. It was an outdoor pool and the stars were amazing in the night sky. I looked up at the heavens and conversed in my heart with God about what was happening in my life. I was still healing and learning how to live for His purposes, and now I felt like He was asking me to let some things go in my life that were holding me back. They were old behaviors that were tied to old beliefs that I was still harboring in my heart. If I were to continue to grow in His purpose I needed to let these go and trust in His direction for my life. So that is exactly what I began to do, starting that very night.

    Ever since our relocation to Missouri, trouble had been brewing for a while. The kids were approaching school age now, and a decision had to be made as to where they would reside so that they could go to school. Having the kids traveling interstate from one house to another every other week was not going to continue to work. Attorneys were hired and we both squared off for a full blown custody battle over the children. This is exactly what I had feared months before would happen, and now it was becoming a real-life nightmare.

I had been trusting in God and His promise that He had made to restore me and my family. I knew that having the children live with me was the better choice for them. I was also determined to let God use this circumstance to continue to develop my faith.

The process leading up to the trial lasted for months. By the way the trial was going, I was sure that I would be awarded residential custody of the children. I was reading my scriptures. I was praying multiple times a day. My friends were praying for me. I had dedicated my life to allowing God's will to direct my steps. I was doing everything right. I knew I couldn't lose. What could possibly go wrong?

After months of preparation, litigation, and several thousands of dollars in attorney's fees, the ruling was finally in. I anxiously awaited the call from the attorney while on the job in Missouri. I was extremely hopeful, but I quickly realized that this was not going to be good news at all.

After all that pursuit of righteous living, God had allowed the court to award residential custody to their mother. I was given liberal visitation time with the children, but that is not what I expected. I felt like Abraham on Mount Sinai with his son Isaac, especially that moment right before the Lord said to remove Isaac from the altar of sacrifice. This was of course because Abraham had not withheld from God his only son.

The difference here is that God did not take Abraham's son in that moment of sacrifice, but He did allow the court to take my children even though I felt like I was doing everything He had asked of me. I was so devastated that I had to leave work immediately after hearing the news.

The pain was so deep, so penetrating. I didn't think I could bear it. It was there in the depths of my despair that my heart cried out to God, questioning why. I cried out to Him in desperation, *"Where are you God? Do you not see what is happening here? Why won't you save me from this situation? Why have you forsaken me in my time of need?"*

Before I was a true believer and real follower of Christ I never cried. I was too tough and always on guard. After I gave my heart to Jesus, he did something to my heart. He made it soft again. He made me more sensitive but that was not helpful in this situation. For days I cried out to God. I cried out in disappointment. I cried out in sadness. I cried out in anger. I simply cried.

I did everything He asked me to do. I did all those things on that list that the crazy old lady made me write down. I prayed my heart out. I truly trusted in Him. He was supposed to be restoring me and my family like He had promised!

I had seen people angry at God before, and I never understood how someone could get so angry at the creator of the universe especially when He could just crush you like an ant. I had never been angry at God before, but this *ONE* time in my life I was angry with Him.

As if the job loss, failed marriage, and destroyed business wasn't enough, the court was placing my kids in an environment that I knew wasn't going to be right for them and God didn't do anything about that. Why did He forsake us like that? Is this the reward for being obedient and following God's plan for your life?

As difficult as it was in the days following the ruling, I decided that despite how I was feeling about this, I was going to continue to trust in God's plan for my life. I wasn't going to allow my situation to dictate a circumstantial faith. I knew that what He was doing in me and my family was greater than anything we had ever known. Slowly but surely, a miraculous peace began to return to me over time and I knew that things were eventually going to be OK.

A Girl Called

In their hearts humans plan their course, but the LORD establishes their steps.

~ Proverbs 16:9

    The problem with raising yourself is that by the time you're a teenager, you feel like you know everything. You believe you know what's best for yourself, even more so than other teenagers. When you've lived your first fifteen years the way I did, you quickly learn not to trust anyone, much less trust their advice. My life forced me to depend on myself because there was no one else I could rely on.

    Up to this point in my life I really had no guidance. What I was taught about life came from school or from the Independent Living Program I attended as a teen in foster care. They taught me how to open a can, how to change a tire, how to balance a checkbook, and how to prevent steam burns when pouring boiling water. They taught me a few practical life skills that would normally be taught by a parent.

What they didn't teach me was how to be a good wife or mother. They didn't teach me how to trust people, or how to allow someone to get emotionally close to me. No one taught me how to properly express my feelings, or that it was even okay to do so. No one taught me how to manage my past or how to truly heal.

While in foster care, I attended therapy and counseling sessions. But these sessions centered more on talking about the things that had happened in the past and the things currently happening in my life. We discussed some of my feelings about those things, but we never talked about a true recovery. I needed direction and tools that would help me recover from a life time of trauma. It was as if merely discussing what had happened to me with a therapist would in some way eliminate all my mental, emotional and physical scars.

I needed so much more than someone to hear me. I needed someone to teach me how to be a healthy person. I was a wounded, broken child who desperately needed to know what normal was and how to become an adult, not just a child who pretended to be an adult. I needed help to discover that I was a person of great value and worth. I needed to know I deserved a normal life. My self-image was so warped that all I saw was damaged goods, unworthy of happiness or normality in my life.

When I was around fifteen years old, a crisis at the foster home where I was placed had left me looking for another place to live. Because of the lack of foster homes in my small town, I was left searching for another option. Not only did I find a place to live, I ended up finding a home and a family. I was allowed to live with my best friend who I now call my sister. Her parents took me in, and treated me like I was their own child.

For the first time, I had someone who gave me rules and consequences for breaking those rules. They provided structure, unconditional love, and even laughter. More importantly, they gave me the freedom to be a child. No longer was I expected to be the adult decision maker. While other teens would rail against their parents for giving them responsibilities and consequences, I cherished these things as an expression of love. It was something that I was missing, yet I never even knew it.

After I graduated from high school, my new sister and I decided to move into an apartment in the city where we both attended college. We worked, attended school, and enjoyed the independence of living alone together.

For me, this was a completely different kind of responsibility than when I lived with my birth mother. This was something I chose for myself and not something forced upon me. Plus, I had someone who shared in the responsibilities and parents who checked in on us often.

Shortly after my eighteenth birthday, I got married. I saw it as the next logical step towards adulthood and age was not a consideration. To be honest, I saw myself as a thirty year old woman in an eighteen year old body. I was eager to start a family and become everything my parents were not. I would be a great mother with a great marriage and have a wonderful loving home. I was determined to never make the mistakes my parents did.

I was married for a little over a year when I had my first child, a beautiful baby boy. We had moved to a great new city and we had, what I considered, an upscale apartment. My husband had a great job, so I didn't have to worry about money for the first time in my life.

Just two years after our first son was born, we had our second son. We were able to afford a townhouse and upgrade our cars. We even began to replace our hand-me-down furniture with newer furniture and really turn our house into a home. My life was beginning to feel like the dream life I always envisioned.

After five years of marriage, things were beginning to become difficult. I was living for my kids, my work, and quite frankly, for myself. Looking back, I don't believe my husband and I had any idea how to be married, or how to be parents, or how to make changes for the better.

Furthermore, my poor self-image was reinforced with every negative statement my husband flung at me. It wasn't long before my marriage became miserable for me and I began looking for a way out – an escape. It seemed easier to divorce than to fix the giant mess we had created.

My friends at the time didn't encourage me to stay married either. They continually said things like, "You deserve to be happy!" What they meant was if I'm not happy, then get a divorce. Even my Christian friends told me God wanted me to be happy. They reasoned I couldn't be a very good mother to my children when I was so miserable. Most of my friends even said God probably had someone else planned for me, someone better to marry. They said I probably had a soul mate that I had missed.

A few older people in my life tried to help save my marriage by giving us advice and by coaching me.

They shared with me God's plan for a marriage and the roles of a husband and a wife. To be honest, this wasn't helpful mentoring at the time.

In my heart I felt there was a God out there. Part of me even wanted to please Him. But, that desire was overshadowed by my view of God as the ultimate Supreme Being who didn't care about me. If He had He would never have allowed people to abuse me, or my parents to abandon me. Instead of taking care of me, He let me live a life of incredible misery.

I began to question those who mentored me to turn to God. The old feelings of being unable to trust anyone surfaced. I pushed away the advice of those who were strong Christians who had already walked a similar path, and instead accepted the advice of the friends who called themselves Christians, but manipulated God's word to make it fit the situation.

In hindsight, I can see I should never have rushed into marriage at such a young age. I should have waited and worked at becoming a healthy, whole, and complete person before ever entering into a serious relationship. I should have explored Christianity and developed a relationship with God before pursuing a marital relationship. Looking back, I don't think I understood what the marriage vows that I took truly meant.

From the outside looking in, you would have never known I was struggling with enormous pain and self-loathing. I never realized just how deeply the abuse and neglect I had endured had affected me. Nor did I realize it would continue to plague me as an adult.

I struggled constantly with allowing people to get emotionally close to me. I cringed and cowered when someone raised a hand jokingly. When my husband talked down to me, or when we argued, I immediately put him in the same category as my abusers. I closed down my heart to him.

Outwardly, I looked strong and happy. Those who knew me always saw me as a happy person and one who was quick to make others laugh. Even those closest to me had no idea that inwardly I was extremely fragile and filled with self-loathing.

I was emotionally shallow, never allowing myself to invest too deeply in feelings with those closest to me, besides my children.

My husband and I finally divorced after six years of marriage. I moved back to the town where I graduated from high school. I wanted to be near my foster parents and raise my children in the small town I had grown to love. I also wanted to get away from the friends and coworkers who knew me as a divorced failure. I was looking for a new beginning.

Moving back to my hometown was not the fix I anticipated. I was embarrassed that I was now divorced and a single mother. Divorced. Single Mother. Two titles that I felt were only more marks against me; more reasons to feel unworthy.

One night while hanging out with my friends, we stopped on our way home for a quick dinner. While we were eating, I noticed a sign on the front of an old movie theatre across from the restaurant's parking lot. It was now a church. I drove past the restaurant and church every day on my way to work. Somehow, I had never noticed the church before that night.

On this night, something grabbed my attention and tugged at my heart. I suddenly felt drawn to the church. It was almost like it was calling me to go there. I couldn't explain the feeling and I didn't mention it to my friends. Because of my history and my doubt about God, I simply couldn't bring myself to check it out.

Every time I considered visiting the church, I thought of all the reasons why I shouldn't go there. I was a divorced single mother. Surely, the people there wouldn't want someone like me around. I didn't know anything about church. I didn't own a Bible. I wouldn't know what they were talking about if they read from the Bible. I didn't have church clothes, whatever that meant. But worst of all, I was a broken person – too broken to go to church. No one in that church would have a past like mine.

Months went by. Each day when I drove past the church, I turned my head and looked at it. Even though I didn't visit the church, I couldn't escape feeling drawn there.

One year, over my kid's spring break, I decided to visit Australia by myself. I had a few friends in Sydney and Melbourne who invited me to come and visit. Since my boys were with their dad, I decided to make the twenty-seven hour trip to Sydney. Bleary eyed and exhausted, my friend met me at the airport and took me to dinner. Even though I was exhausted and struggled to keep my eyes open, I was so excited to be there.

The trip was a once in a life time opportunity. As a child, I never dreamed that I would travel. I wanted to do everything and see everything. There were so many things to see and explore, the days flew by in a whirlwind. It was a wonderful experience, and it became a memory I will cherish for all of my life.

As my trip neared the end, I spent the evening listening to one of my all-time favorite music artists sing and play at the Sydney Opera House. The music had affected me in a way that is difficult to explain. It was as if the memories of the pain and hurt I had experienced since childhood were brought forward, and rather than relive the hurt I could finally examine the feelings objectively.

After the concert, I felt like I needed to walk and let whatever was affecting me work itself out. I strolled through Hyde Park completely oblivious to all the touristy landmarks around me. I felt as if I were in another world. It was a world far away from everyone and everything that had hurt me. Wanting to explore the feelings more than the city, I wandered away from my friends and walked through the park alone.

I strolled past Archibald Fountain thinking about my past and the many mistakes I had made. I began to feel melancholy as I thought about how far away my children were at that moment. I thought about how I failed them by getting divorced. I sat down on the steps of Saint Mary's Cathedral and looked out toward the park. The city seemed surprisingly empty.

As I sat staring into the city, the melancholy feeling slowly began to turn into an overwhelming feeling of peace. A warm sensation slowly came over me, as if someone was pouring warm oil on the top of my head and it flowed over me. The feeling of peace and joy ran over my body and went deep down into my bones. I was unable to move or speak.

Then I heard a voice. A voice I had never heard before yet knew instantly. The voice spoke so gently, yet firmly, saying, "Why do you run my child? You run and you run, but you always run into Me."

In that moment, I *knew* there was a God in Heaven who reigned over the world. I knew that He loved me, because I could feel the pain in His voice. He wanted me to turn to Him, but all I had ever done was run. I ran from my past. I ran from people who loved me. I ran from God and the calling He had for me. Yes, I was called, yet I ran.

From that moment on things began to change for me. I started listening and paying attention to God whenever He spoke to me. I observed the world around me, and began feeling different about it all. I began to have deep compassion for other people. I wanted to do what was "right", though I didn't exactly know what that was. I even wanted to let down my guard and trust people, and most importantly, trust God.

Yes, I felt called, but I didn't know what I was called to do. Where and how was I to begin?

On the flight home I began to doubt what I experienced. Did I imagine the whole thing? Somehow,

I knew instinctively that answer was no. I knew God had spoken to me. But what if I told someone what had happened and they didn't believe me? I had to admit, it all sounded a little crazy.

When I played it over in my head, I realized it had to be God. He knew about my running from Him. He knew I was scared and that I didn't trust Him. Clearly, He was trying to get my attention; to show me I didn't have to run anymore. He wanted me to know that there was a reason worth staying.

When I landed back home, I was a new person. I was someone who wanted to know more about God and what He had in store for my life. I called the only Christian friend I had who went to church regularly.

I was nervous about telling her what happened. I didn't know how she would react. In my world, people who hear voices usually end up in an insane asylum. But when I told her my story, she said, "Wow, that's going to be an amazing testimony!"

I had no idea what a testimony was.

Now that I was home and getting back into my normal life, I needed to figure out what to do next. I knew the place to start was at the church God called me to months before. Completely jet lagged, and with no idea what to expect, I took my boys with me to the church.

I had a feeling of being very much at home, but completely outside my element. During the worship music, some church attendees raised their hands and sang with deep passion. I saw tears in their eyes as others held their hands close to their hearts and bowed their head while singing. They seemed connected to God through worship, and I hoped I could one day have that connection too.

During the sermon, the pastor used words like "fellowship," "Holy Spirit," "discipleship," and "evangelical." Even though he was speaking English, I struggled to understand what he was saying. I felt like I did in Australia when locals confused me with words like "brekky," "arvo," "uey", and "pressie".

Despite my slight confusion and inability to follow everything that the pastor said, I still felt called by God. I was at the right place, and this was the right time. At the end of the service, I prayed the sinner's prayer. I gave my whole heart, my whole mind, my whole body, and my whole soul to Jesus Christ. I finally made Jesus my Lord and my Savior.

Afterward the pastor said, *"When a person gives their heart to Jesus, all the angles in heaven cheer!"*

Suddenly, the entire church erupted into applause. It felt good to be a member of God's Kingdom and their cheers were an encouragement to me. When I walked out of the church that day, I felt like a new person. As they say in our church, I was born again as a new creation. It was time for a whole new life.

Even though I had attended church a few times as a child, attended off and on before I got married, and tried to go to church when my boys were babies, I never had a relationship with Jesus. To be completely honest and transparent up to that point, I faked it.

The pastor of the church where I was married preached so much about what I shouldn't do, I soon tuned him out. The church I attended for a short time while I was married was just a way to have a social community and to look good to other people. I wasn't there to have a relationship with Jesus. Looking back, I realize during my brief time in church wasn't a complete waste. God was planting seeds of faith.

When I became a believer and a follower of Jesus Christ, I found that I had a desire to get as close to God as I could. I went to church with my children as much as I was able to. I got involved in several groups and classes, and even volunteered in the nursery.

I was extremely ashamed that I didn't know what my new pastor meant when he mentioned certain people in the Bible. He would say, "Everyone knows the story of Joseph..." and based his sermon on that fore knowledge. But, I didn't know the story of Joseph. I didn't know the story of Jacob, or Job, or Mary and Martha, or Jonah . I didn't even know the difference between the Old Testament and the New Testament.

My lack of knowledge never deterred me from trying to learn. Instead of feeling defeated, I took detailed notes. When I went home, I studied my notes and discovered what the sermon was really about.

As a new Christian, I sincerely believed I would now live a happy life with no problems larger than being stuck in traffic. Unfortunately, I was wrong. In fact, I quickly learned just the opposite was true. When the enemy of our soul realizes we're suddenly on God's team, he does his best to get us back. He attempted to use my old thoughts and feelings of being damaged goods and unworthy of anything normal to keep me broken.

For me, the real test of my faith was an internal battle most people never knew I was fighting. Outwardly, I still appeared happy and outgoing, but on the inside I constantly struggled with self-doubt and self-loathing. With it I battled the urge to run and to sabotage.

Emotionally I would run away from close relationships, and use my new found faith as an excuse to keep my distance. I told myself I was unworthy of a relationship with a guy because I was a divorced single mother. I reasoned any relationship would be too complicated and take time away from my kids and from growing closer to Jesus.

I assumed that most single men had great childhoods, loving families, and an all-around perfect life. While I, on the other hand, had already made a terrible mess of my life, and struggled to move past. I didn't feel attractive because my body was scarred from years of physical abuse. Even my heart was scarred from lifelong emotional and mental abuse.

My faith seemed further tested as God began opening doors for me to participate in ministry work. He gave me compassion for widows and orphans. He called me to missions in Africa. He spoke to my heart again and again saying one day I would be a pastor and speaker used to help thousands of people.

I heard God and I believed Him when He said He wanted me to do these things. But, I also knew I couldn't. I argued with God that pastors are not divorced, single mothers. They certainly weren't women who had a story of abuse like mine. I argued that I couldn't take my children to Africa as a missionary, even if He made a way for me to go.

I didn't believe in myself, so how could I expect anyone else to believe anything I had to say. How would anyone ever listen to me share God's Word, especially when I was still learning myself?

What I didn't understand when I became a Christian was how God deals with the past. He washes our sins away and throws all of it into His Sea of forgetfulness. Never again will He hold it against us. In fact, He gives us a new beginning, and even better, an opportunity to use our past as a testimony of God's mercy and grace.

Slowly, I began to learn that when we accept God's mercy and forgiveness, we also accept His sufferings. Jesus says that those who follow Him will suffer as He did, be hated and despised. But He also says not to be afraid because He has already overcome the world and Satan for our sake.

He expects us to trust Him as we take the bad with the good. In a sense, we become soldiers in a very real battle; a spiritual battle for our soul. Soldiers walk through difficult, dangerous, and even life threatening situations for a purpose. When that purpose is complete, soldiers feel blessed to be able to serve and achieve that purpose.

Christians don't always see the purpose of the trials and difficulties. Nor do we always understand why we go through these things. But, we know from God's Word that whatever comes is a test of faith. As our faith is tested it is being perfected.

It is through our faith in Jesus that we endure hardships, yet, still have a heart full of joy. If we choose to walk through the trials, we'll be tested, but we will come out victorious on the other side.

Boy Meets Girl

Take delight in the LORD, and he will give you the desires of your heart.

~ Psalm 37:4

For several months after relocating I was leading a Divorce Care ministry in our local church. I knew that God was calling me to serve. I just didn't know exactly where, and I thought this was a good place to start. When I started this ministry in our church, I didn't want anyone to have to go through the pain that I experienced in divorce. I had hoped that I could somehow help them avoid that pain by making better choices, or at least encourage them to go through it with God's help.

As God was healing my heart, I got to the point that I knew He had more planned for me. I felt like I was ready to move on from this particular ministry I was leading and take on something new, but what? I was ready to move on from divorce and begin something new.

Deep down I also knew that the plans that God had made for me would involve being remarried someday. I began to pray about this every day. I wasn't in any rush to the wedding altar, so I told the Lord if He had someone in mind He would have to bring her to me. As I sought and took delight in Him, He gave me the desire for my wife. He knew the qualities that I was looking for in a wife. He was the one who put those desires in my heart, and He was the best person to bring her to me.

I looked at some of the local churches for a singles group to get to know more people who shared similar values, but it was hard to find one and we didn't have one at my church. The singles group from my last church was really great and I had high expectations. It seemed like I wasn't getting anywhere and I thought to myself, "If I don't find something soon, maybe I could start a group of my own."

One day I found a singles group at another church that was actually meeting together and doing fun things. Since I was considering starting a group of my own, I decided to contact the coordinator of that church's singles group. When I called the church that sponsored the group they gave me a contact phone number. I called the number, and after no answer it went to voicemail. It was a girl's voice and I left a message for her to please return my phone call.

Sometime later I received a call from Katherine. When I answered the phone I told her that I was curious about starting a singles group in our church. I wondered what they were doing at her church and thought it might be fun to see if we could join forces. She said they did several things including a regular sushi night, but that week they were also going over to a friend's house for a little "get-together". I wasn't so sure about the sushi because a friend of mine scared me off years before, but she sounded cute so I decided to come and meet her and the gang at their friend's house.

This was going to be interesting to say the least. Here I am going over to someone's house that I don't know to hang out with a bunch of single people that I've never even met before. Oh, by the way did I mention I had my two preschoolers with me? After I rationalized that what I was doing wasn't *completely* ridiculous. I figured it would be OK. I was just wanting to hang out with some fun people for the evening. It wasn't like I was trying to find a girlfriend or anything. This was all for *research*, right?

When I arrived at the door I mentioned that I was looking for Katherine and we were able to introduce ourselves. It felt a little awkward at first, but hey there was a purpose in this, right? She was very sweet to me and quickly set me at ease. In fact, her two young boys were already outside playing in the back yard so I wasn't the only one with kids that night.

I quickly realized that we were the oldest singles in the group and the only ones with children. Some of the people there were members of the church's worship band and they played music and sang that evening. It was really quite fun. Katherine and I actually shared some good moments getting to know one another that night and she invited me to hang out with them again. The next time they would meet at a local favorite sushi restaurant...I accepted the invitation.

I was still recovering that week from the news I received about the kids, and now they were going to begin school in Oklahoma without me. This weighed heavy on my heart and I mentioned this to my new friend, Katherine.

As time passed, we got to know one another very well. We became fast friends and I was actually enjoying sushi for the first time ever. We talked about many things including what we thought God said regarding relationships.

It was very refreshing to see someone who had very similar ideas and interests as I did regarding the

Kingdom of Heaven. Most single people our age seemed to be more interested in *not* staying single as fast as they could. I was definitely more interested in slowly finding someone that matched up with the desires I had prayed for in a wife. God was still restoring me, and it seemed that He had sent me someone who cared about what I was going through.

Once we started becoming closer, I endearingly began to call her Kate. One day we talked about that "nickname" I started calling her. I mentioned that many characters in the bible who were called to do great things for the Kingdom of God had their name changed. It marked a moment in their lives when they were set apart by God. I suggested that she start going by Kate because that is exactly what was going on in her life, and I really liked that about her. Needless to say, that name stuck.

The cool fall weather crept in and the holiday season was coming upon us. Kate and I weren't officially dating or even courting yet but we were seeing quite a bit of one another. I really enjoyed our time together, and I was looking forward to getting to know her on a deeper level.

Christmas was around the corner and there are so many wonderful things to do in the Ozarks of Missouri. I had been to Silver Dollar City before, but never during the holidays. I've always enjoyed seeing the Christmas lights and my kids love our tradition of viewing them every year. But only being in Missouri for a short period of time, I realized now that we were finally able to see the Christmas Lights at Silver Dollar City. I decided to have Kate come with us. I asked her to take pictures of the kids and me, but I think hidden deep down I was also going to enjoy her company as well. What's more romantic than hot cocoa and Christmas lights, right?

Looking back it makes me smile to reflect on the process we went through to get to know one another. We took the time to discuss the calling of God in our life and what that was going to look like in a marital relationship. We discussed what we prayed for in a spouse, and believed that God would give us the desires that He put in our heart. We developed a friendship based on trust, love, and respect for one another. It was time to take things to another level.

With Christmas rapidly approaching, it brought an excitement on our journey of getting to know one another. We began falling for each other, and we weren't quite aware of just how far. We wanted to be sure and intentional about where our relationship appeared to be going. We were also very cautious. I decided that I wouldn't even so much as kiss her until we were sure to be in a committed relationship.

I can still remember the exact moment that I fell in love with Kate. I had always known her to be a very compassionate, loving, and of course fun person. She was genuinely interested in learning more about me. She also cared for others with great tenderness. I had just been through some rough times and she always seemed to know what to say or do to make me smile. This was significant because I knew her story too. It was also a difficult story, but she always found a way to let the sunshine into a situation.

It was Christmas Eve and we were having a great time together. We were becoming very close and the Christmas spirit only exceeded our exuberance. We were also looking forward to spending time with my children tomorrow. As time went on that evening it became very late and about time for me to leave. In fact it was just after midnight so it was actually Christmas.

Out of the blue, I was notified by my children's mother that her plans had changed. Suddenly she told me that if I wanted to get the kids at a decent time in order to attend the plans that I had for Christmas day, then I needed to meet her immediately. It was a one and one-half hour drive from where I was, so if I was going to get my children for Christmas I had to leave right then.

I was furious. I already had the entire Christmas day planned out, and this was my scheduled time with them. I had made all my arrangements and plans according to the court ordered visitation. Many people do not realize the mountain of effort it takes to coordinate family plans when it comes to visitation, especially over the holidays. Maybe if they did consider that, they might spend more effort trying to keep their marriage from ending in divorce.

Sure, I could put my foot down and demand her compliance, but she wasn't that cooperative and especially now. I didn't want to jeopardize missing even a single moment with the kids at Christmas, even at the fault of someone else. Under protest, I decided to meet her right then to pick up the kids as she demanded.

When I got off the phone, I'm sure that Kate could see that I was visibly upset. When I told her what was going on, she was very compassionate. I told her that I had to go and get the kids right then, even thought it was in the middle of the night.

She knew I was upset about this unreasonable situation, but her compassion for me really comforted me. Kate asked me if I would like her to go with me. I knew this was going to be a major disruption, not to mention the loss of sleep for both of us right before waking up early on Christmas morning. I didn't want her to have to go through that with me, but I couldn't refuse her offer.

I had an overwhelming feeling of love for her that could not be contained. I had never told her I loved her. I thought we were both moving in that direction, but neither of us had ever said those three sacred words to each other.

I can't explain exactly how I was feeling at that moment other than I could tell that she was saying she loved me without ever uttering a word. I couldn't help but express my love for her in that moment. We embraced, and I softly told her that I loved her. Even though it was in the midst of adversity, this was one of the most special moments in my life that I will never forget.

I knew that I had finally found someone who was made for me. The one woman that God sent specifically for me, just as I had prayed for. I knew that she would be a wonderful helpmate to me on our future journey of marriage and ministry together.

In the months following Christmas we began a courting relationship. It was more than dating, it was building a relationship with the intention of marriage.

We wanted our relationship to be an example to others. We knew our children, friends, and family were watching, and we wanted to make sure that our relationship was an example of God's glorified plan.

In our continuation of seeking God, we also grew closer to one another. We dreamed of how God would use us someday in His ministry plans. We were soon to be married and we wanted our marriage to have meaning and purpose. Our marriage ceremony and subsequent honeymoon was absolutely wonderful. It was a true gift from God.

It was the most peaceful and happiest time in my life. The presence of God surrounded us as we escaped to the mountains of Colorado for a week. God was blessing us for our faithfulness to Him, and we were truly able to have a mountain top experience on our honeymoon.

Girl Marries Boy

Hold on to instruction, do not let it go; guard it well, for it is your life.

~ Proverbs 4:13

There was something exciting about living for God instead of myself. It meant there was a whole new world to learn about. My lack of Bible knowledge had been embarrassing to me, so I began to read and study everything I could find. It was as if I had been wandering in a dry desert starving and thirsty, and almost instantly I was now in an oasis. All I had to do was bend down to drink, and reach my hand out for food.

One of the books that I read was about dating and preparing your heart for marriage. The things I read were amazing to me. It was information I never had thought of before, much less heard anyone else talking about. I became very passionate about preparing myself for marriage, but also for guiding the others as they prepared for their future marriage.

I began to lead a single young adult group at our church. I wanted us to study God's word and prepare ourselves to follow God's plan for marriage. I wanted us to learn together and to become stable adults before seeking a relationship. I especially wanted this for myself.

In some ways this was probably the blind leading the sighted. Most of these young adults had been raised in church and some were even attending Bible College. They came from a lifetime of Sunday school lessons, and I was a brand new Christian.

Through my studies I learned that men and women are created for relationship, therefore it is natural for them to want to come together. If a man and woman develop a deep friendship, that friendship will often lead to a committed relationship. Dating tells us that we should jump into a relationship before we develop the friendship, but it's through friendship we can truly learn about the other person's character. If we took time to really discover how the other person acts and reacts without the guise of trying to impress, we may see something totally different.

For example, during dinner with several friends you can easily listen and watch for certain things that may seem small now, but will become huge issues later. You may see that the person that you have a crush on is mean or disrespectful to the wait staff. You might realize that most of the things he or she talks about are negative, rude, or even hurtful to others, but disguised as humor. Watching their table manners alone may send you running for the hills.

One of the most important things I learned about marriage and dating is that you really need to be a whole person before you attempt to involve yourself in a relationship. For me, I still struggled with that feeling of being unworthy of any relationship, and I needed to understand that God had healed me. I needed to learn how my history could be used to help others in the future rather than just be a story or a bad memory.

For people who have experienced as much trauma as I have, this is very difficult. In fact, it is an ongoing process that may never fully be complete. It is difficult to understand why someone can't "just get over it" and "just move on". That's like asking someone to put a band-aid on your severed limb, and just get over it.

A little over a year after God called out to me in Australia, I was still attending the church he called me to. I got up early to get my boys ready, and we drove over thirty minutes each week to be there. I was participating in all of the outreach projects, and even photographing them so the photos could be used in marketing later. I worked in the infant nursery almost every Sunday. I also became the leader of our young adult ministry, helping to organize outings and events for us.

In my free hours, I really tried to focus on healing and becoming a whole person. This was something I felt was vital to my future. I was convicted by the things that were coming into my life so I took drastic steps to guard my heart.

The first step was to stop listening to secular music and begin listening to Christian music. The lyrics in secular music were sometimes sad, degrading, or incited anger. Instead I filled my life with music that inspired hope, love, and joy.

Other changes that may have seemed drastic included limiting the movies that I watched to only those that I could let my young children watch with me. I even ended some friendships because I needed to distance myself from their lifestyles.

No one told me that being a Christian meant I had to do these things. I just listened to what God was saying to me, and I knew this was what I needed to do in my life.

The biggest area of my life that I gave over to God was regarding marriage. I really had no intentions of getting married again, yet I didn't want to keep this part of my life from God. Instead of being afraid and running, I let God guide me. I started to pray for God to send a husband to me. I asked God to send a man who put God before everything else in his life, and a man who would respect my views on dating, and be a Godly father to my two boys.

About a year after I had become a Christian, I received a call from a guy named Jerry. He said he wanted to talk with me about the single adult group I led at our church. He had contacted the church to ask about our ministries for singles, and they put him in touch with me. He asked me how our group was structured because he wanted to start a similar group at his church.

After a lengthy discussion about our group and our goals, I invited him to come to an event we were having later that evening. Our group was meeting at the home of a married couple who was taking the time model a Godly relationship. I tried to be welcoming, and I thought that he would want to meet us in person and allow me to show him how our group worked.

Jerry actually showed up a little late because he had to pick up his son and daughter who he brought along with him. I was sitting at the kitchen table with a friend when he came in. She jokingly nudged me and said that I should "marry that guy". I laughed at her and made a silly comment about how I couldn't marry a guy with a daughter because I didn't know anything about raising a girl.

That evening was memorable for more than one reason. Jerry and I got along really well and found a lot to talk about. Our friends later told us they could see a spark between us, but we were both just talking about our new cell phones and other common interests. There was a tornado warning and extreme weather that kept us from leaving until later than we expected. It gave us extra time to fellowship with all the people in my singles group.

Jerry and I continued to stay in touch though text and instant messages. I included him in all of the events that we had, and he was able to come to most of them. Our friends love to say that I had a huge crush on him, but it wasn't like that for me. I did see something different in Jerry that I had not seen in other guys, and it wasn't just in his appearance. He truly seemed to be seeking God and putting God's will first in his life.

Jerry had only been divorced for about a year, and he was struggling through a very rough custody battle. He later confided in me that he was anxiously awaiting an important decision on the custody arrangements around the time we met, but the outcome was not what he had hoped. The judge had given residency of the children to his ex-wife, and he would only see them during his scheduled visitations.

Watching what Jerry's divorce and custody battle had done to him and to his children helped me to understand just how important it is follow God's plan for marriage. If two people meet, fall in love, and marry, they need to have a strong foundation to their marriage.

The majority of marriages I had seen up to that time in my life had built their marriage on emotions. It appeared that their marriage was in jeopardy every time one person felt angry, hurt, upset, disappointed, or wronged.

Emotions change, but God is steadfast. He challenges us to do the right thing, even when we don't feel like it. And let's face it, most of us find ourselves at times not wanting to serve someone who doesn't deserve it.

I believe that the discovery of this, the knowledge of needing God and not our emotions as a foundation in all aspects of our life, was an eye opening reality. All of the people who had told me that God wouldn't mind if I got divorced as long as I was happy, were speaking from emotions.

Jerry wanted to take his children to see the Christmas lights at Silver Dollar City, an amusement park nearby. He asked if I'd like to go with him and I accepted. Silver Dollar City has a spectacular Christmas light display and I had never seen it. The entire park is covered with lights, and some of them dance to music.

Jerry and I took his two children, but mine happened to be away for the weekend so it was just the four of us. The children loved the lights, and they seemed to be particularly excited to have me around. They wanted me to carry them almost every moment, and I was happy to have them near me.

I've always been very motherly and love to take care of people in general. Jerry's children were going through a rough time in their lives. They really needed some extra love and care, and I was happy to provide as much as I could.

I watched Jerry when he was with his children, and I listened to him talk to them and teach them. In my opinion, he was the best father I had ever seen in my life. He wasn't complacent and he did not let them get away with bad behaviors just because he was suddenly a "weekend dad". He taught them to always do right and to aim for the stars. He always put them before anyone one else, except God.

Even though the evening was cold we hardly noticed it because it was so magical. It was this evening together that first opened my eyes to Jerry as a potential future husband. I was quickly discovering that he possessed the traits I had been praying for.

By December, Jerry and I knew that we really liked each other and that we had similar views on life. I was really considering Jerry as the man I would marry, so I began to pray and seek God's wisdom.

I was really concerned with how we would blend our family together because I had already seen some difficulties even in the small things like planning an outing with all the kids. We had to align our schedules so that we had our children on the same weekends, which could be a challenge. Not to mention that suddenly two children would become four children whose ages were only staggered by a year or so.

I really trusted God to guide me, and my fervent prayer was that He would give me a mother's heart for Jerry's children so I could love them like my own. I prayed that I would be a Godly wife, and that my past would not be an issue in my future. I waited for God to answer my prayers.

When I least expected it, I discovered that God had answered my prayers and given me a mother's heart for the children. Jerry's son was particularly sensitive and had anxiety issues stemming from the divorce that were just beginning to show up. One day he got really upset and afraid of a dog and he clung to me asking me to *save* him.

My heart was so compassionate and so protective of him in that moment that I knew I loved him just the same as my own children. I was still a little worried about mothering a little girl, but I learned how to braid her hair, play dress up in princess dresses, and to let her be a daddy's girl when she needed it.

Jerry and I had not quite entered into what we would call a courting relationship. For us, courting meant we were on a path to marriage and we would follow God's path for getting there. We wanted to keep ourselves pure even though we had both been married before, and I know God has blessed us for doing so.

We also wanted to be smart about blending our family and to raise our kids God's way. In hindsight I can see that we were both still pretty new at being Christians, but it was this exact thing that sealed my love for him.

We discussed what marriage would look like for us, and we talked about what had happened in our past. I explained my life long struggle with self-doubt and how I had a habit of sabotaging things out of fear. I even told him how embarrassed I was that I didn't know the

Bible as well as I should, and how I still had doubts stemming from this.

One evening Jerry called and asked if he could come over to give me my Christmas/Birthday present. I lived about an hour away from him, but he said he didn't mind the drive. He was eager to see me, and I was excited to see him also.

Jerry's gift to me was the single best gift I had ever received in my life. It was the dramatic reading of the Bible on CD. Jerry explained to me that he understood that I had struggled with knowing the Bible stories that other people grew up hearing. He thought that I could listen to the Bible on my long drives to work, to pick up my boys, and on my hour long commute to church.

The fact that Jerry put my spiritual health above all other earthly desires showed me what a great spiritual leader he was. The moment I received that gift is the moment that I knew I loved him like a wife loves a husband. I knew that with leadership like his, I could follow him anywhere God led us. Even though I still doubted my worthiness, and knowing that a blended family would be difficult, I wanted to pursue marriage.

We didn't rush into a wedding, but instead we took the time courting and really discussing how marriage should work according to God's design. We knew that where there is no vision, the people parish, so we took the time to create a vision statement for our marriage. Besides the Bible, this vision statement would be something that we could always return to in the difficult times to remember where our marriage is heading.

To follow God's design for marriage meant that we would need to both put God first, then each other. This is particularly difficult for blended families because each person could feel like their own children should come before the marriage.

It's not only difficult to understand, but extremely difficult to put into practice. When you add ex-spouses, past hurts, alternating holiday schedules, and financial complications into the mix, you could be doomed before you begin.

Knowing this about second marriages, Jerry and I really wanted to build our second marriage as an example to others. Whether it was a first marriage or a subsequent marriage, we felt like couples should know that there is a better way.

After much prayer and consideration, Jerry and I decided to use our wedding day to celebrate God's plan in front of our friends and family.

We honored God and put each other first in our marriage by having a simple ceremony in the church. We asked our pastor to marry us with just a few witnesses, rather than a large ceremony. This was our own personal way of making a covenant with God and focusing on each other, not the wedding. After we were married we spent the next week on our honeymoon in a cabin in Colorado. We enjoyed a wonderful time together, exploring and relaxing.

When we returned home we had what we called a Family Union Celebration. Instead of having bridesmaids and groomsmen, Jerry and I walked down the aisle together with our four little children in front of us. When we arrived at the altar we had our youth worship band lead us and our guests in worship, just like church.

This was particularly important to us because we were honoring God and setting an example in front of our friends and family, some of which were completely unchurched.

During the service, we asked our pastor to help us form a unity jar with colored sand. Each of our children had picked a color of sand to represent them.

Jerry and I also had our own colors. We had all six bottles of colored sand set up in little bottles next to a much large one.

Our pastor first poured a bottle of white sand into the large jar and explained that this was to represent God, who would be the foundation of our marriage and family. Jerry poured his sand in next as our pastor explained that God intended the man to be the leader of the house, the protector, and the provider. I poured my sand in next as he explained that the wife is equal to her husband, yet should still submit to his authority as unto the Lord.

Each child then poured their sand color by order of age, oldest to the youngest. Finally, the pastor poured the remaining white sand over the top and explained that it represented God's covering over our whole family.

From the moment Jerry and I made a covenant with God to become husband and wife, we knew our marriage would be different. We were set apart by God to do great things. We both felt called to help others with their marriages.

For Jerry, I would say that this call came even before we were married. For me, the calling was there but like always, I wanted to run from it. I continually doubted that anyone who had been divorced would be respected and listened to as they taught about marriage.

    This time, however, I now had a partner who would encourage me and build me up so that I could do what God called me to do.

More Trials

"But if serving the LORD seems undesirable to you, then choose for yourselves this day whom you will serve, whether the gods your ancestors served beyond the Euphrates, or the gods of the Amorites, in whose land you are living. But as for me and my household, we will serve the LORD."

~ Joshua 24:15

Kate and I loved each other deeply, but blending two independent entities into a cohesive family unit was going to be quite a project. We were all getting along and blending as perfectly as possible. Everything was new and fun and we really enjoyed one another. Once the newness began to wear off, the blinders came off as well.

We went through the typical issues that I'm sure most blended situations encounter. I think we handled them pretty well. After experiencing fatherhood for the first time years ago with my firstborn, I realized how being a father had changed me forever. I was hooked, and it touched my heart to hear someone call me dad.

One day we sat all the children down and told them that we weren't trying to replace anyone's mother or father. We explained to them that their birth parents will always be their mom or dad and nothing could change that. We also told them that they could call us whatever they were comfortable with, as long as it was respectful of course.

I was looking forward to being a father again and parenting these two boys that had come into my life when I married Kate. This is where some of the trouble seemed to start as it does with many other step-families. The dynamics of all our relationships appeared to be blending quite nicely until the other parents noticed how close our family was beginning to bond. We continued to press on raising our children up the way God had intended, but from time to time challenges arose especially when we offered our ex-spouses differing opinions in parenting styles.

We approached life with our family head on. Kate and I were both working full-time jobs. We were attending our home church and getting involved in just about everything we could. We were trying to find our place in ministry. We got involved in several projects helping out the church.

Our house was located in a small town about thirty miles from our jobs, and even further from our church. So just about every day we were driving nearly one hour to get to work, or an hour to drive our family to church. We were definitely in the midst of the grind when trouble hit.

When my two youngest children went to live with their mother following the recent custody dispute, I was given liberal visitation rights. I knew how important having a father in their life was going to be. Even though I lived over one-hundred miles from their legal residence, I wanted to make sure that I had an active presence in their lives. They were very young at the time and so every single day I made an attempt to call them on the phone. I wasn't always successful in getting through to them on the phone, but nevertheless I called daily. I also committed to staying involved by communicating with their teachers at school and tried to stay connected that way as well.

One day I got a call from one of their teachers and it was not good news. This person began to tell me that my child had disclosed allegations of abuse that happened in their mother's home. I was stunned. It was every parent's worst nightmare.

She continued to tell me the details of the incident as I stood there paralyzed by a flood of emotions and questions racing through my mind. By the time the call ended I was in full-on protection mode. I had to do something, but who prepares for this kind of news? Nevertheless, I talked with Kate and decided I would jump in the car and rush down to investigate for myself.

Prior to hearing this news, I had recently left a great place of employment for a seemingly better employment opportunity. I was lured by the promise of more training, better opportunities, and of course an increase in salary. I didn't realize this at first, but the new employer was not very family friendly. Now, I was finding myself asking to take the day off to attend to family matters across the state line.

I spoke with some trusted people regarding the allegations of abuse, prayed, and ultimately retained an attorney. I filed for a change of custody as well as emergency orders to be put in place while custody would be decided.

I was confident that action was going to be taken to ensure the safety of the children. In fact, after a few days the children were court ordered to be removed from where they were, and placed with me. It was a bittersweet moment. On one hand the children were safely with us, but on the other hand we had to face the aftermath of this traumatic situation.

Things quickly went from bad to worse. After what happened, I never thought I would have to return the kids so soon to that situation, but that is exactly what was ordered.

We just couldn't understand how this could possibly be. They claimed that there were *safety precautions* put in place to ensure their safety, but of course I was not convinced. What could I possibly do about this, it was an order of the court? I felt so helpless and abandoned in the situation. I continued to fight for the children but I didn't realize that we were already doomed.

Months after the ordeal began, the case seemed to be deteriorating before my eyes. There were so many people involved. They were all opining about what they *thought* was going on. The facts all started out so clear, but *somehow beyond our control* they were being morphed into some big cloudy mess by those who were supposed to be helping us. I couldn't understand why they couldn't see the truth of this situation when it was so clear.

I had to take so many days off of work and it was affecting me in a negative way. I was fighting for my children's lives, and it seemed like no one cared except for me and my wife.

Right in the middle of all this we received the news that Kate's biological mom was very ill. We flew down to Texas to see her in her last days. At first she seemed to be improving, but when we were boarding our flight back home we got the news that she had passed. We were emotionally drained at that point, but we made plans to return for the funeral.

A short period later, we were told that Kate's grandmother and also my grandmother had passed. We attended one funeral locally, and the other one was located in New York.

Of course this meant that I had to take more days off of work, and all this time off was not boding well for me. In fact, shortly after these series of events, my employment decided to lay me off. I had such high hopes of opportunity, but unfortunately all these family emergencies had not helped our situation. This was very untimely because I thought we were getting to some pivotal moments in this case.

To make matters worse my attorney was recommending to me to drop the case because she said that there was no likelihood that we would win. The case had so deteriorated that overcoming the obstacles needed to change custody seemed practically impossible. We could continue the case, but any further legal involvement would cost several thousands of dollars that I simply did not have. We had already asked everyone we knew if they could help us financially when this started, but all those wells we turned to were dry. Of course now that I was unemployed, any significant lump sum payment to an attorney was impossible and just like that...the case was dismissed.

It basically came down to the dissolution of the actual truth, and the lack of money. We were helpless and abandoned. Again. Wasn't God watching this injustice? Why wasn't He stepping in and pulling us out of the pit we were in?

I felt like the Joseph in the bible. Here God gave him this glorious dream, but what happened? He was thrown into a pit and became a slave to his circumstances. That's what we were, a slave to our circumstances. We couldn't do anything about it, or could we?

God made me that promise that He would restore me and my family, but when was that going to happen? He had the perfect opportunity right here. How much longer would my children have to stay on Abraham's altar?

Even though we were assured safeguards were in place, I was more vigilant than ever to stay in contact with the children.

Just as unexpectedly did devastation came to our home, did a surprising employment opportunity come knocking. The catch is we had to relocate immediately. The good news was that it was closer to the kids in Oklahoma. After being out of work and going through what we went through at the time, by the grace of God were we able to purchase a house and move into our new home.

Things were settling down a bit, and we decided that Kate would focus on homeschooling our children instead of returning to work. We now had a beautiful home with some acreage that was all ours, and we were so blessed to be there. The burden was still heavy on our hearts for our other children, but we were learning to trust God with that situation.

We decided to focus on exactly what God wanted us accomplish in our lives and we were going to trust Him with the rest. Eventually Joseph was set free from his prison, and he was restored to a place of honor after his continued faithfulness to the Lord. That is something we had to look forward to, I just hoped it wouldn't take as long as it took for Joseph.

We were continuing to pursue life with purpose and we wanted to do things God's way. We spent tireless amounts of our own energy and power in the past with the hopes of favorable outcomes from the fruit of our own efforts. Things were going to be different now. We truly wanted to make choices within God's will for our lives, and not just *say* that is what we were doing.

We wanted to make a conscience and intentional choice to do things according to His will not only for our lives, but also for our family. Even though we went through some extremely difficult times, we wanted to trust the final outcome with the Lord and that He would take care of us all.

Now that we were living in a new city, we were looking for a good church to attend. We just couldn't seem to find one that fulfilled us like our last church, but we were determined to get spiritually fed. After much consideration in prayer we decided that we would return to my old church across the border in Oklahoma. This was going to be another long drive to church every week, at least forty miles each way actually. Luckily it was all interstate travel.

We had been seeking the Lord for direction in ministry. We continued to explore the calling on our life towards marriage ministry. We didn't know exactly where that calling was taking us, but we were soon to find out.

On the day we returned to visit my old church we made a new friend. His name was Leo Godzich and he was one of the founders of the National Association of Marriage Enhancement. He preached a bold message that day about honoring marriage in our community and spoke of the desperate need to help couples in our area and around our nation.

That Sunday they were also dedicating a new building that was opening as an outreach to the community's married couples. I told Kate this was what we were waiting for. There was no coincidence in what was happening today. We were very excited to be present for the celebration of the open house for their new building dedicated to saving marriages. We wasted no time inquiring as to how we could help out.

Before we knew it, several weeks of training had flown by, and we became certified in the NAME counseling network. Time after time we got to see firsthand how the Holy Spirit touched the hearts of these precious couples. It was truly amazing and extremely energizing for our own marriage as well. Even the training was beneficial to our own marriage. We didn't realize at the time how valuable that instruction was going to be in our future.

We were getting even hungrier to learn more about God so we continued to dive into our bibles on a daily basis. We decided to begin studying for our minister's credentials. We knew that someday we wanted to speak boldly about God's plan for marriage, and we needed the knowledge and wisdom to do it.

One of my favorite things to do was listen to some of my favorite preachers on satellite radio, and I found myself studying their different styles of preaching. Who knows, maybe someday this would come in handy! We were choosing to serve God with all our heart and He was preparing us for something big.

Finding Happily Ever After

"But to you who are listening I say: Love your enemies, do good to those who hate you, bless those who curse you, pray for those who mistreat you."

~ Luke 6:27-28

Have you ever heard the phrase, "And they lived happily ever after"? Most of us have heard it and we have also dreamed about it. We set our expectations of our future based on the feelings of love we experienced during the dating days.

Whatever "happily ever after" was meant to look like usually turns into something more like treading water and just trying to keep your head up so you can breathe. In my experience, happily ever after is what you make of it.

The first few years of our marriage were particularly difficult for us all. Jerry's previous marriage was generally a hot button topic. While I had a mother's heart for his children, I didn't have a mother's voice in the decision making.

When you are the step-parent, you may love the children and want the very best for them, but legally you have no say in anything. The emotions that accompany the lack of power you feel will forever surprise you. This is something that you can't teach to someone who is about to become a step-parent.

I had no idea how frustrating and emotional this would be for me even though I had heard and experienced stories of blended family drama many times before. God sees my mother's heart but the court definitely does not.

Jerry's ex-wife seemed to make things more difficult than they needed to be when it came to the children. Even the smallest little thing seemed to get blown up into a huge issue. I did not appreciate the way that his ex-wife treated him or even me, yet I couldn't say anything without making Jerry feel torn between us.

I could see that Jerry wanted to figure out a way to diplomatically handle the difficult situations with his ex-wife, and yet he wanted me feel at peace with the decisions he made. Jerry always did what was right. I, however, struggled with the decisions that he made because doing the right thing didn't seem to be fair.

Things were never fair.

One of the many examples of this was early on when we were still dating. Jerry was informed that if he wanted his children for his holiday visitation, he would have to drive double the normal distance in the middle of the night. His only alternative was to miss his holiday time with his children, so he gave in and made the trip.

Travel time in general was not fair either. Rather than meeting half way between the two homes, Jerry was forced to drive an additional thirty to forty-five minutes for each pick up and drop off. The drive was so long that it put a strain on our family time together. It seemed that by the time he was home with the kids, it was almost time to take them back again. We would lose so much time with Jerry and the children, yet there wasn't anything we could do about it without creating a huge court battle.

Another thing I learned early on in our marriage is that when one parent is being unreasonable regarding the parenting plan outlined by the court, the only other recourse is to file something with the court in an attempt to make them comply. This entails hiring an attorney and spending thousands of dollars. Then you will wait for weeks and sometimes months at a time for the attorneys to file motions and communicate back and forth until a court date can be set.

By the time you actually go to court, the judge is nothing more than annoyed that the two parties could not work things out on their own, and both leave unhappy with the final ruling.

After only a year of marriage, we came to a crux and we felt like we had to do something. We were already swimming in debt from Jerry's previous custody case, but it was more than just the annoying issues that we faced. Suddenly the children were alleging abuse in their mother's home and we had to protect them.

The children alleged abuse in their mother's home multiple times to several people who documented it. We knew that with these reports and documentation that the judge would certainly want the children to be removed and placed in Jerry's custody.

For me to follow God's plan for my life, I had quit my high paying job as a Project Manager for a popular eCommerce company. I was finally able to fulfill my call to Africa by working in the Africa's Hope Missions office at the General Council of the Assembly of God.

Because I took a reduction in pay in my new job, our budget was extremely tight so we had to take drastic steps to proceed with a custody modification. We sold every thing that we could sell in order to raise enough money to pay for an attorney. The attorney all but assured us that after reading the reports, the judge would most likely remove the children and place them with us. We put all of our faith and trust in this attorney.

When the judge finally heard the motion for emergency custody and interviewed the children, he did exactly what we had hoped. He ruled that the kids would come home with us. They told us to enroll them in school, and prepare for them to stay.

We were overjoyed to say the least. It felt exactly how justice should be, swift and always looking to protect the children.

Our joy could not last very long because the wording of the judge's ruling left a loophole for the children to return to their mother's home. Not much more than a week after they came home, we were told to let them go back to their mother when she came for them.

For me this was unthinkable. These children were alleging abuse, yet somehow the system that was designed to protect them was failing.

Now, our attorney told us that there was no way we could win this case. She said that even if we wanted to proceed, it would cost thousands of dollars more, and the outcome would be the same. She convinced us that at this point there was nothing we could ever do to get the children moved.

Generally speaking, I never let too many things drag me down and I am naturally positive person, but this was a crushing weight for me to carry. Almost every visit the children would now comment on some type of alleged abuse they had suffered from the days before.

When Jerry and I talked about anything relating to this difficult subject, one of us would end up so emotional that we often became just as frustrated with each other as we were with the situation. We were dumbfounded that our attorney was so very confident in the beginning, but quickly changed her story. Her words, "there is no way you can win" rang in my ears. We were powerless and in some ways hopeless. Yet as parents, how could we just sit by and do nothing?

I began to wonder if I had made the right decision by marrying Jerry. Before we were married I had very little drama and lived mostly carefree. Undoubtedly, I had experienced stress as a working single mother, but I had far less drama in my custody arrangement.

Now my entire life and marriage seemed to be chaos. I wanted to raise children free from the hurt and the pain of child abuse that I had known, and yet here we were facing what I had vowed to prevent. I couldn't believe that I had put myself into such a horrific situation, and one where I felt so helpless to do anything.

I felt like the joy had been sucked out of my life. I regressed to memories of how God had abandoned me as a child and left me in such miserable situations, and now He was doing the same with these two children that I loved so much. I never once doubted the all-powerful, loving, graceful God I had come to know and love. Never once did I question my salvation. I just could not see past the situation or how anything good could ever come of it.

During the time that we fought for custody of two of our children, our other two children and I lost valuable time with Jerry. We were newlyweds with a new family, trying to find our way together, yet there were large blocks of time when it was as if I was a single mother again.

Jerry was constantly traveling from our home in Missouri to attend to court matters Oklahoma. Not only did this affect those of us at home, but his work started to suffer. He had switched employers in order to earn a larger salary for the same work he was already doing. However, this company did not value family the way his previous employer did. They resented that he had to take so much time off for court matters, and eventually laid him off.

We were already struggling with the rollercoaster of emotions from the custody case, and now pressure was added with Jerry's job loss. As the saying goes, when it rains it pours.

Not only did we have this custody battle, and job loss, but we also lost three family members all within a few days of each other. First my biological mother died, then my grandmother from my adoptive family, followed by Jerry's grandmother. These losses, on top of the feelings of loss that came with the children returning to their mother, were unbearable for me.

When I look back on the months and months of fear and anxiety over the safety of the children, I realize that I was not putting all of my trust in God and His divine plan. I still wanted to control things in my own power, and I did not spend near enough time in prayer.

I was constantly looking for a way to fix things, rather than focusing on how God was going to be glorified no matter what. If it had not been for the missionaries that I worked with and the time they spent in prayer, I would have fallen apart completely. They were truly our prayer warriors, holding us up when we were too tired to battle anymore.

Our prayer warriors became mentors who also helped me grow in my Christian faith. I had only been a born again believer for about two years, and I still had a lot of rough edges from my past.

One of my mentors reminded me that my feelings were temporary. I shouldn't base long term decisions on temporary emotions. She knew how hard this custody case was on my marriage, and her advice kept me grounded firmly in my faith despite what second thoughts popped into my head.

She also reminded me that I prayed for a mother's heart and God heard that prayer and He answered it. He would answer my prayers and bring them home one day, if I could only hold on long enough.

Shortly after we were forced to withdraw our custody modification, God blessed Jerry with an amazing job. I had mixed emotions about the new job because it meant that we would have to move an hour away from our current home.

On one hand we were moving much closer to Jerry's children, but on the other hand we were moving further away from my family, and the only school my children had ever known. I was also very nervous about leaving my support system at the Africa mission's office, trying to find a new church, and how we would establish ourselves in another city.

This move turned out to be the first step in God's amazing plan to answer my prayers.

Our entire lifestyle changed as we moved out of our tiny home and moved into a huge home with land where our kids could explore. We could cultivate a vegetable garden, pick fruit from our own trees, and wave at the cattle as we drove down the road to our house.

We decided that now that we had moved I would not return back to work. We also felt that this would be a great time to begin homeschooling our children. Through homeschooling and our friendly neighbors, we were able to make friends quickly and get involved in our community. I started to feel like our life had stabilized and we were becoming somewhat of a normal family.

After visiting many churches near our new home, we realized that we couldn't find one that was a good fit for us. Ultimately we decided to attend one of the first churches where Jerry had felt at home after he became a born again believer. The only problem was that this church was almost an hour away from our home. We would even have to travel across the state line into Oklahoma and pay a toll fee just to be there.

I was skeptical attending a church where Jerry had been before, but it turned out that the drive was more than worth it. This church was unlike any I had ever attended before.

The Holy Spirit overwhelmed the congregation any time they were together. The prayer warriors from this church are some of the people we still call on today when we are in need. At this church, God opened the doors for us to step into ministry in ways we had never thought possible.

On October 10, 2010, our church had a particularly powerful morning service in which the Holy Spirit seemed to be working in each and every person. It was so incredibly influential that our pastor just allowed the congregation to continue to worship, each in his or her own way.

The worship band played softly for over an hour as people remained in worship. To describe this moment to a pre-believer is to describe the moment that your child is born. The powerful love and emotions that overwhelm you are actually indescribably in that moment to a non-parent.

I knelt down on the floor of our church and felt God's powerful presence wash over me. It was as if someone slowly poured warm oil over my head. I could feel it consuming me as it washed over my whole body.

As I prayed, I drew into a smaller ball as if doing so I could somehow get closer to God. I didn't want anyone to touch me for their touch might break into my moment with Jesus. Then, for the second time in my life, God spoke to me in a voice that I could hear as clear as day.

His words to me were, "No longer do I want you to say 'the children do not live with us'. I want you to say, 'They are coming home soon.' For I am about to do a great and mighty work, and I will bring them home soon."

I wrote His words in my journal, and I told Jerry about it near the end of the service. He said he could tell God was doing something amazing in that moment by how peaceful I became. He had wanted to know what was happening, but he didn't want to disturb the moment.

After I showed him my journal, we were in awe that God would hear our prayers, speak to us, and now go to battle for us. We prayed together and thanked God for what He was about to do. We praised Him for His kindness to us.

I believed what God had just said to me, and I began to build a strong faith around it. I was so honored that God would speak to me, and there was no way I would question that He was answering our prayers to have the children come home to us. Even if I didn't understand what was happening, I would trust.

Jerry and I decided that while we waited for God, we would work as hard as we could to prepare ourselves and to pursue the ministry God had called us to. I dove into my studies and worked alongside my children doing my own school work as they did theirs. I read the entire Bible in less than three months, and spent several hours in prayer and devotion each day.

Jerry and I began working toward our minister credentials with the General Council of the Assemblies of God by attending Global University. We also became Certified Marriage Specialists with the National Association of Marriage Enhancement (NAME) and volunteered as marriage counselors at our church.

In general, life felt like the "happily ever after" that I had dreamed of when Jerry and I first got married. Our marriage was stronger than ever, and we were serving alongside each other in ministry. Our two children who were at home with us were flourishing in our homeschool environment, becoming smart and responsible preteens.

We still experienced drama relating to custody matters, and we were always concerned with the welfare of our other two children. However, we were able to have peace and joy in the difficult times because we were spiritually armed, and better able to handle anything that came our way.

In April 2011, about six months after God had spoken to me; Jerry called me and said that he received a strange message regarding the children. He was also denied access to the children for one of his visitation weekends. There seemed to be no reasonable explanation given.

We were very concerned and worried that something horrible had happened to the children. We both began to pray for God to intervene in the situation, whatever it was, and to protect the children. Jerry later received information that the children were again making allegations of abuse.

I still remember standing in our kitchen talking with Jerry about what we should do. I reminded him that God told us He was bringing the children home soon, and this was how He was going to do it.

We hated to go back to court again, yet we trusted that God would fulfill His promise to us. We dreaded the emotional and financial drain that another custody battle would cause, yet we went forward boldly. This time we had no fear because we knew that God was for us.

Jerry began to travel to Oklahoma and set things in motion for the custody change while I remained home with the other children.

Being the step-parent in these situations is one of the most difficult roles a person can take. You will find yourself stuck between wanting to support your spouse, wanting to protect your spouse, and wanting the very best for your children.

The court does not care about your opinions other than when you testify as a witness. Most attorneys who specialize in family law have already heard most of these stories from their past clients, so they really just want to cut through the drama and talk about the facts.

You'll also find that in some cases you may not agree with what your spouse and attorney have decided to do, yet you have to find a way to speak up in a way that doesn't sound demeaning, or like every other crazy step-parent the attorney has met.

Almost every day there was some new horrible news that would have been devastating had I not had faith that God was with us on this. It was almost comical. The more we discovered that yet another thing was stacked against us, the more we thanked God for what He was doing.

We knew that God was not just going to hand the children over to us, but He was making sure that the whole world knew that He did it. He was going to show the world that the only one who was in control of the situation was God Himself.

The first bit of bad news was when Jerry discovered that the attorney who had represented us previously, was friends with his ex-wife. Not only that, she had also represented the husband of Jerry's ex-wife as well. We also discovered that the Guardian ad Litem that was assigned to our case was operating from a position of conflict of interest. We also found out that Jerry's ex-wife, opposing council, and the first judge on the case were serving together on a church ministry board. At this point we began to question everything about our previous case in this court.

All of the people involved wielded powerful influence in our case, and it appeared they were all unjustly set against us in spite of the truth. In the natural, there seemed no way to overcome these insurmountable obstacles.

Jerry continued to drive to Oklahoma often for court hearings and meetings with his attorney. It was apparent that God had orchestrated our move to the area just so we would be closer to the children and to the court.

I stayed home for most of these hearings and only attended the ones where I was required as a witness. From home I helped as much as I could, and even uncovered some of the evidence that was later used in the case.

I didn't let the case consume me. Instead I was constantly praying. I was not asking God to intervene, but I was thanking Him for what He was doing in our situation. My most fervent prayers were not asking God to do something for us, but rather praising Him for what He was doing.

With the information that we had regarding the court and the apparent bias against us in our case, you could expect our natural reactions to be anger, hate, dismay, outrage, frustration, and overall dejected. This is not how we felt.

There were times of outrage or frustration, but they were quickly turned around by the knowledge and faith we had in the final outcome of this trial. We walked in forgiveness daily, and rather than be angry with the actions of others, we felt sadness and pity for them.

I had every right to be angry and frustrated, yet I simply wasn't. I had a peaceful and joyful spirit almost all the time.

The trial seemed to be constantly moving one step-forward and two steps back with little to no progress. There were times when I sat in the hallway of the court house for hours waiting to be called as a witness, only to be sent home without testifying.

In the previous case, these hours of waiting at the courthouse were filled with dread and anxiety. Now I used the time to read a book, knit a scarf or socks, read and journal from the Bible, and pray.

I found that journaling the Beatitudes, from Matthew 5:3-12, was particularly comforting for me. In these scriptures I learned that God called me blessed to be insulted and persecuted. He called me blessed for being merciful and meek. He called me blessed for being persecuted.

I marveled at how I could feel like I was blessed to be walking in these trials. In the past, I resented what was happening to us in court because I was living in the moment and in my emotions. But this is what faith does; it allows the same person to have a completely different perspective when faced with the same circumstances.

The Greek word for "blessed" in these verses of Matthew 5 is makareeos, which means supremely blessed, fortunate, well-off, or happier. Jesus was saying that you can be happy even in the difficult times. Happy in times when you hunger or thirst, when you are persecuted, when you are poor, when you mourn, and even when others revile you.

He teaches us that those of us who are seeking to be better Christians will often be wronged in numerous ways, but we can choose to be happier and call ourselves blessed because ultimately we will see the Kingdom of Heaven.

One particular verse of the Beatitudes, verse 8, says, "Blessed are the pure in heart; for they shall see God." The word "pure" in this verse comes from the Greek word katharos which means clean, pure; physically purified by fire.

In order for our hearts to become clean, they must be purified by fire similar to how gold is purified. During the refining process of gold, the gold is heated by fire to temperatures of over one thousand degrees. As the gold melted, a craftsman would stir the gold and skim out the impurities that rose to the top.

1 Peter 1:7 also uses the imagery of our faith being tested and refined through fire similar to how gold is tested and refined. I came to the realization that in order to have a pure heart and to live blessed and happy, we would sometimes have to go through trials just like our current situation.

Even though Jerry and I were walking through fire, we knew that the outcome would be the blessing God promised. Not only would we be "blessed" as the Beatitudes taught us, but we would come out with a pure heart. That is truly "happily ever after".

Truth and Purpose

"You intended to harm me, but God intended it for good to accomplish what is now being done, the saving of many lives."

~ Genesis 50:20

Our lives were moving right along with relatively no *visible* bumps in the road. It was almost peaceful. On the surface everything seemed fine, but a parent knows when things aren't quite right. Being separated from two of our children for such long periods of time began to take its toll on me. Many times I was unable to contact them and I began to worry.

We carried on with our ministry work and pursuing our studies as well. We felt like so much time had been wasted in the past on what we needed to accomplish. We had a plan that no matter what opposition came our way, we were going to accomplish our goals in ministry.

We had a great support system of friends at not only our *local* church, but several friends within our ministry network. There were many times when someone boldly spoke encouraging words to us at just the right time. I believe that God himself was using them to strengthen us with His words in our time of need. He was preparing us for what was about to come.

There were many important moments of decision in my life that I can remember. Up to this point, two of those moments that stand out to me were marked by someone bold enough to come forward and let God use them to speak directly to me. These moments were a fork in the road. They were times when I needed to change course, make a decision to take action, and not continue what I had been doing.

The first moment that stands out to me was years ago when that old lady gave me that to-do list. I still laugh when I think about that moment, but I did those things I was called to do. It forever blessed my life and influenced the man I am today. Before I met her I was at a standstill and seeking direction from God. After our encounter I was on a mission.

I decided to make the changes necessary in my life in order to prepare myself for what God was going to be doing. I wasn't sure what that was exactly, but the Lord was building my faith and I was willing to please Him.

The next moment was even more significant. I don't know if it was because the message I would receive came from my beautiful bride, or because of the heavy challenges we were facing with the children. You see we had been crying out to God to move in our situation. We were begging Him to make changes in this situation because what we saw happening with the children was not good.

I remember thinking, if, as a husband and father, I was responsible for the spiritual health of my family, I needed to have the authority to act. I needed God to place me in that position of authority. How was I ever going to accomplish what he wanted in my family if my children weren't even living with me full-time? I constantly cried out for Him to do something about this.

Every day at church was a good day, but this particular day we had a wonderful church service. God was moving throughout the entire church that day. Then it happened. He spoke to my wife and He had a message for me.

It was 10/10/10. God is so funny sometimes. He knew I liked numbers, and I can't help but think I have a Father that takes interest in the smallest of details. He made sure that I would remember exactly when this moment came.

The message was that the children were coming home to me soon. He had heard our cries and now it was time to put that energy into building our faith. We were no longer going to be crying out in desperation on this issue with the children. We were to step out in faith and begin to thank Him for the work He was going to do.

This was a shift in our way of thinking. This was going to require us to boldly believe He was going to bring them home to us. We were to cultivate our heart with the thoughts of faith that we knew to be true.

A few months later disaster struck our family once again. One day while preparing plans to pick up the children I was told that things had changed and that I would not be seeing the children that weekend. There was some sort of emergency, and that I would not have access to the children. This was odd. I inquired as to the details of this situation since it conflicted with my scheduled visitation, but I was not given an answer.

Several days later, still no answer and even though I reached out to them, there was no communication from the children. This was getting ridiculous. I was ensured by court order to have a daily phone call with the children, and this wasn't even close to being honored.

We were coming up on the weekend when I finally heard from the children's mother. I was informed that she was refusing to let me see the children for yet another weekend. This was more than I could bear. Something had to be done to stop this nonsense.

I jumped in the car and headed to Oklahoma. It was time to get to the bottom of this. I drove to the office of my attorney who handled my case not too long ago, but she had moved. I found her new office and went inside. I saw the Guardian ad Litem from our case there and thought that was strange.

I asked to speak to my attorney and proceeded to go into her office. As soon as I saw her, I told her that it was starting again with the kids and I needed her help. That is when I found out that she was friends with my ex-wife. Shortly after this, I found out that she also represented my ex-wife's current husband in a custody matter. Once again, I was stunned. How could this have happened? I left her office immediately in utter shock of what I had just been told.

I drove around looking for someone to provide some help to me and my children, but there was seemingly no hope. I went to the school to see if I could find some answers in what was going on with the kids. I talked to the counselor, and was once again shocked at what I heard. More abuse allegations that had taken place in the mother's home. Not long after hearing this news, I discovered that the Guardian ad litem assigned to the case had been performing her duties under a position of conflict of interest.

I was reliving the nightmare from years before once again. I cried out to God, "What are you doing?" Immediately, I thought about His promise months earlier. Despite the turmoil I was going through at the time, I was comforted in that moment.

I found an attorney who would take the case. We initiated legal proceedings right away, but right off the bat we were met with opposition and delays. We tried to get the children placed with me on an emergency basis as we did before, but because of a legal technicality that had just recently been made into law, we were unsuccessful in doing so. This fight for the children's safety was not going to be won quickly. In the weeks following I began to notice that the truth was slowly beginning to come to light.

We prayed every day that the truth would come out. We were beginning to uncover years of information that we had not been aware of. I was amazed at what we found out. We became aware of several conflicts of interests with various parties regarding our situation. We were desperately seeking the truth, and slowly but surely God was revealing it to us in a methodical way.

Although it felt like we were going through another familiar tragedy in our family, something was different this time. We were learning to lean on our trust in God that He would take care of things.

I happened to watch the movie "Facing the Giants" one day in the middle of all this mess. It touched my heart in a way that complimented the message that God gave to me months earlier. In that message He wanted us to have faith that He was at work in this situation, and that we were also to have faith that the children were coming home to us soon.

In the movie, the main character faces a seemingly insurmountable obstacle of adversity. He makes a choice to change his methods of coaching with the purpose to glorify God. Furthermore, he instructed his team that no matter what the outcome was for the football game, they were going to praise the Lord for His glory whether they won or lost.

I found this to be a particularly interesting concept for exercising my faith. We were all in and I couldn't think of a better way to build our faith and at the same time get God's attention than praising him despite our trials. It got to be a rather comical moment between Kate and I, because before every hearing or important court-related event we reminded each other and would say, "If we win we'll praise Him, if we lose we'll praise Him."

God was really doing something wonderful in our hearts. He was protecting us in a miraculous way. During this particularly rough time in my life I began to rely on several scriptures to guide my daily journey and get through each and every day.

2 Corinthians 10:5 says, *"We demolish arguments and every pretension that sets itself up against the knowledge of God, and we take captive every thought to make it obedient to Christ."* I was bombarded by negative thoughts related to our situation.

I could have easily let these thoughts overcome me and take over my heart, but I compared them against this scripture, Philippians 4:8 *"Finally, brothers and sisters, whatever is true, whatever is noble, whatever is right, whatever is pure, whatever is lovely, whatever is admirable—if anything is excellent or praiseworthy—think about such things."* If what I was thinking was not true, noble, right, pure, lovely, admirable, excellent, or praiseworthy, I would turn that over to God so that that He could deal with what I could not handle.

I didn't want to take the chance and let any untruth enter as belief into my heart. Luke 6:45 says, *"A good man brings good things out of the good stored up in his heart, and an evil man brings evil things out of the evil stored up in his heart. For the mouth speaks what the heart is full of."* This had a tremendous effect on my mind, my heart, and my life in general.

I was truly transformed and strengthened by these daily exercises in faith as mentioned in Romans 12:2 *"Do not conform to the pattern of this world, but be transformed by the renewing of your mind. Then you will be able to test and approve what God's will is—his good, pleasing and perfect will."* With these keys to success for His perfect will in our lives we were preparing for the long battle ahead.

He wasn't just preparing us for what we would inevitably face with the children, He was preparing us with the battle-tested tools and skills that we would share with others that we came in contact through our ministry. The principles we were learning in our adversity were miraculous and life giving.

Month after month would pass away at a snail's pace and we were no closer at resolving this. Our faith in the promise that the children would return home kept us going through all of the challenges and many setbacks we faced. We faced delay after delay, and we just wanted to bring the truth to light in court.

At one point we alleged that there were some obvious conflicts of interest in the case, but those details didn't seem to matter. In fact, opposing counsel and the Guardian ad Litem in the case joined together in a motion to try to suspend or force supervised visitation for me and the kids.

I couldn't believe the audacity of their claims, but I quickly realized this was going to be a difficult battle ahead. Despite the attempts of their motion to limit my contact with the children, it went nowhere. The judge even granted me additional visitation during this period. A small victory, but the tough work was still yet ahead.

Something that had concerned me for years was my son's lack growth progress. He was very small for his age, and it was noticeable to everyone who came in contact with him. Making matters worse was that whenever I had to take my son to the doctor, they too would comment on his poor growth progress. They would explain to me that he should see a pediatric endocrinologist.

I brought this up to his mother several times, but not much appeared to ever get done. With all the court action taking place, I was trying to find a way for his growth condition to get addressed. The problem is that getting an appointment with a medical professional in that specialization was an extremely long wait. We called a few of them, but each were a few hours away in any direction.

In the midst of all this chaos, one day my son was playing on the monkey bars at school. He fell from them on the playground which resulted in a broken arm. When I heard the news, I rushed to the hospital. They wrapped his arm and told us that there wasn't much they could do for him since he needed to see an pediatric orthopedic specialist. I told his mother that if she would let him come home with me that night, I would take off work and take him to get his arm set the next morning.

As we were finishing up setting and casting his broken arm, I got a call from Kate. She said that the endocrinologist's office just called and they had a cancellation. They said if we could get there in the next couple of hours we could take that appointment and establish our son as a patient. This was a miracle in itself because I never would have been in the position to take him to this appointment on such short notice.

Over the next couple of months our son was poked and prodded in just about every conceivable way. The result: no medical explanation for his lack of growth. We asked the doctor how this could be. He explained that every test that I took him to get always came back in the normal range. He said there was still one possibility for his lack of growth and it was due to psychogenic factors. Due to the documented issues of anxiety related to problems in his mother's home, the doctor gave him a working diagnosis of psychosocial dwarfism. This was an environmentally induced form of failure to thrive that typically results in a lack of growth in children.

Once again, I was stunned. What was the course of action to rectify this situation? Change the living environment for at least six months to see if there is an improvement or catch-up in growth. We went for a second opinion, but we received the same story. We even approached a third doctor with this information, and they all agreed that placing the children with their father would be their recommendation.

Surely the court would see this new evidence and act quickly. Sadly, that was not the case and it only made the fight to protect the children and bring them to our home even more fierce than ever.

The delays also continued which were heartbreaking because my son was losing his valuable yet limited time to catch up on the growth he had lost over the years. We finally knew what was causing his lack of growth and had a plan to treat his condition, but we were helpless to get that plan implemented.

We tried filing an emergency motion and bringing our evidence before the court, but it seemed as if what we were saying was falling on deaf ears. A trial was finally approaching after nearly a year of waiting, but it didn't really bring any comfort because of how things were going.

It seemed so obvious to us what the truth really was, but people were either unable or unwilling to see it for themselves. Here we were with all this evidence of what was happening. We knew that what we were doing was right, but it didn't appear to make any difference to anyone. It seemed absolutely hopeless…again, but we were still praising God for what He was going to do, and we were not going to give up.

We were continuing to experience what we thought was an unfair bias in the case by the court so my attorney confronted the judge about it. A few days after this tense, but significant moment, the judge did admit that he must recuse based on his feelings that he could be biased against me in this case.

This development was shocking and absolutely blew my mind. What happened in the days and weeks that followed continued to put me in awe at the majesty of what God was doing for us. We knew that walking in the steps that the Lord had ordered for us would yield blessings for our family, but we had no idea the scope at which He would impart His blessings upon us.

Nobody's perfect, but we genuinely wanted to make sure that we were demonstrating an honorable example of what a Christ follower would do in our situation. We wanted people to know that we weren't going to sink to a level that was unworthy of our cause. If we would have done things according to our fleshly desires, that would not bring God the glory in what He was doing in this situation. So we continued to let those godly principles guide us on this journey of adversity that we were facing.

Because of the extraordinary circumstances regarding our case, it began to get a lot of attention. After the first judge recused himself, two other judges got involved. A new trial date was set and we began preparing for the upcoming battle in court.

About this time, God orchestrated another miracle on our behalf. It happened just before the long awaited trial began by way of an investigative reporter. She contacted us and said that she had received information from an anonymous source regarding our trial and that she would like to interview us.

I was very skeptical, and I informed her that we would need to speak with our attorney before any interview would take place. The reporter said that she already had all of the information and the facts to write her story. She also said that story would be written with or without our input. Reluctantly and with our attorney's blessing, we agreed to meet and tell our side of the story.

On the first day of the new trial with the new judge, our story was published on the front page of the Tulsa World for the entire state of Oklahoma to see. All my skepticism was put to rest when I actually saw the truth that was printed.

It seemed that those who were fighting against us were furious when they read the news. We felt like God had worked an incredible miracle that now exposed the truth and conflicts that were going on with our case. It also brought an increased accountability in the case because now there were reporters following our story. I was also very pleased that they printed that we were relying on our faith in Christ to turn things around.

Things got even crazier. After a marathon session in court that kept us late in the evening at the courthouse, the current judge was asked by opposing counsel to recuse herself. As if things weren't tense enough already, this definitely escalated things significantly. More importantly, it also risked the timeliness of the trial.

Now we had to deal with all the legal ramifications of this request for recusal, and we were certainly going to lose additional valuable time. We had already been waiting several months for our moment in court, and now this happens. All I could think about was, when is my son going to get the care he needs for his condition that is made worse by every passing day?

A district court judge ruled that the recusal was going to be granted in order to expedite things in the best interests of the children. So, yet another judge was assigned to the case. Newspaper reporters were in the courtroom to report this district judge was absolutely furious that the opposing counsel would even request such a thing.

With this new judge and a quickly scheduled trial date, we were finally closing in on justice once and for all. We still had many obstacles to overcome, but the truth was finally coming out in the courtroom. We were finally able to have a level playing field and an opportunity to tell our story.

I was amazed at how the truth came to light. It was what we had been praying for all along and it was finally happening. We had been pressed in on all sides, but never crushed. God persevered with us every step of the way. After a few more weeks of waiting, the ruling was finally in and I had one more step of faith to take.

Even though God said *soon,* litigation had dragged on for about a year now. It was taking a toll on me in many ways, and specifically with my job yet again. The company had laid off some employees where I worked. Since I had taken so much time off to take care of my son and all these court matters, my job was suffering. I was afraid I might be the next one to be let go.

After my testimony was complete in the case, I had the time to begin calling around to secure some job references. I spoke to my old boss of the company that brought me to Missouri in the first place. I asked him if he would be so kind as to give me a reference for some job opportunities I was taking a look at, and he agreed. He also said they had an opening on his team if I was interested. I hadn't considered moving back, but I was definitely curious about that possibility.

The next thing I knew, I'm having a job interview, and immediately they extended an offer to me. I stood there in amazement at another crossroads. In one direction the door was open with possibilities abound, and in the other direction the door seemed to be closing before my eyes.

I briefly thought to myself, *what if the upcoming ruling isn't favorable to me, what would I do then?* This job meant that we would have to relocate back to where we were several years before, which was quite a distance away from the children if this didn't turn out the way I expected. This could certainly complicate things. I had to dismiss that negative way of thinking. I knew this opportunity came from the Lord, so I decided to take a leap of faith and I accepted the job.

A few weeks had passed, and I was still waiting to hear a decision on our case. All we knew is that we should hear something within thirty days after the trial had ended. The days seemed to crawl by slowly. The waiting was absolutely excruciating.

Finally, within just a few days of starting my new job, I heard the news. I almost couldn't believe what my attorney was saying. He said that I was awarded sole legal custody of the children. I went out back behind my office and shouted for joy! God had done what He promised He would do.

In the months following, we had some various legal squabbles regarding all of the children that proved to be extremely challenging and very costly. In the end we knew what our purpose was, and we knew that when we walked in God's purposes with forgiveness in our hearts there wasn't anything to be afraid of.

Reflecting on these past moments of pain, physical exhaustion, and financial strain, I realized that the only promises that come to pass are the promises that you allow to come alive in your heart. This will be through believing in faith that God will make it happen through you according to His good and perfect will.

Receiving the Promise

Therefore, my dear brothers and sisters, stand firm. Let nothing move you. Always give yourselves fully to the work of the LORD, because you know that your labor in the LORD is not in Vain.

~ *1 Corinthians 15:58*

    The number of people who prayed for our family during our court case is simply astounding. We were very careful not to tell anyone the details of our case, yet they all knew that we were battling the courts for the sake of the children.

    Just before our story became a headline in the newspaper, our Pastor's wife said something to us that gave us the strength to keep going when everything was coming against us. She probably had no idea the impact her words would have. Or maybe she did, which is why she said them. That was just how she was. Her own faith was inspiring to us, and we knew that when she prayed for us, God heard her.

    During our worship time at church we sang a great song that I always found very moving. This day was a little different because the song seemed to have a more powerful meaning. Part of the lyrics we sang said "that if our God is for us, then who could ever stop us, and if our God is with us, then what could stand against us." The Pastor's wife turned around and pointed at us and she said, "That's for you guys."

She was so right. God had told us that He was bringing the children home, and He was going to do just that. Not me, not Jerry, not an attorney, not a pastor, and not the court. God would do it, and who could stop Him? We didn't have to worry about all of the conflicts of interest with the people involved in our case, because God was for us and who could stand against us?

Something we all should know by now is that God's timing is not always our timing. When God said the children were coming home soon, we thought that meant within a few months. Our custody case in Oklahoma, however, had already dragged on for almost a year and we seemed no closer than we were before.

Author C.S. Lewis writes, "I am sure that God keeps no one waiting unless He sees that it is good for him to wait."

To think about the miracles God performed, and the work that He did in my spiritual life, I know that this waiting was for my own good. While I waited I pushed myself harder to become a strong and faithful Christian. I learned to control my emotions, and when things didn't go well I could give the whole thing over to God. I learned that there is no peace apart from God.

Shortly after the newspaper article made headlines, the court case got very serious very quickly. After so many painful months of waiting, we were about to finally have our day in court. I was excited to testify because this was truly a time when the court would take into consideration what I had to say. However, testifying can be very scary and nerve wracking if you don't have the peace of God. The evidence could be seen by watching the other people in the hallways of the courthouse, each waiting for their turn to appear before the judge.

Our attorney probably thought that I was an insane, wacky, Bible thumping Jesus freak (which I guess I probably am!). Whenever he brought us bad news, or said he was concerned about something that was not going to go our way, I simply told him that we had no need to worry because God was bringing the kids home.

When he delivered bad news, Jerry and I would sometimes laugh out loud and explain to him that we had yet another chance to prove God was in control. He would sometimes rant and rave and curse the people that were giving him a difficult time. We would remind him that no matter what, we loved our enemies, and wanted them to come to know God out of this situation.

In Romans 12, the Apostle Paul writes to the church to remind them that Jesus said to love your enemies. He writes, "Do not take revenge, my dear friends, but leave room for God's wrath, for it is written: 'It is mine to avenge; I will repay' says the Lord. On the contrary: 'if your enemy is hungry, feed him; if he is thirsty, give him something to drink. In doing this, you will reap burning coals on his head.' Do not be overcome by evil, but overcome evil with good."

I have lived and breathed these verses for the majority of my Christian life, yet it doesn't always come easy. Knowing that God has a plan to reach His people through all circumstances, and knowing the love that He has for all of His children creates an atmosphere for me to love and forgive more than I could on my own.

After we had our trial, we had more waiting to do. The judge did not render his decision for what seemed like weeks. I was certain what the ruling would be, yet this anticipation was such a tough thing for me. I've never been very great at waiting, and I think God was working on me in this area at this time, and frankly He may always be working on me when it comes to waiting.

Because our son was diagnosed at the time with Psychosocial Dwarfism, we knew that every day the court took to decide the case was another day that could permanently damage our son. He was already so far behind in his growth, and we just wanted to get him treated as quickly as possible.

While we were waiting for the verdict, Jerry came home with some unexpected news. He said that he received a call from his former employer, the extremely family friendly one, and they wanted him back. Without hesitation, I said he should take the job. The company was so good to us in the past, and I just felt deep down that moving back to our home town was a part of God's larger plan.

In my heart I knew that God moved us closer to the children for the trial, and now that it was over, He was moving us back. While I was sad to leave our friends, our church, our homeschool support group, and our community, I felt like this was the next step in our ministry.

After much prayer and discussion, Jerry called and accepted the job. Just as our excitement about this new adventure was setting in, we got a wonderful phone call. It was within days of Jerry starting his new job that we got the favorable decision in the custody case. Our attorney told Jerry to go and pick up his children, the judge had ruled that they would now live with us.

You can probably imagine our excitement and the emotions that overwhelmed us in the moment we heard the news. God had done exactly what He promised! He brought the children home to us. Not only did He bring the children home, but He used our family and our story to change lives along the way. Our family and friends who prayed with us rejoiced in our victory as we gave them the news.

One emotion that we did not expect is the deep sadness that filled our hearts. As a mother, I could only imagine what the judge's verdict meant to Jerry's ex-wife. The same news that sent us cheering and rejoicing surely filled her with sorrow. We hated that she would have to feel this type of pain and my heart ached for her. No matter how much conflict and hurt we had between us, I wanted God to comfort her. My prayer for the next several weeks was that God would do exactly that.

Over the next few months God showed us that He was not done working miracles in our lives. In the past, we had to travel to Oklahoma or Arkansas to see our son's Pediatric Endocrinologists regarding his growth. At the same time that God was moving us home, He also moved a Pediatric Endocrinologist to our home town. We were able to establish our son at his practice and begin treatment right away.

Jerry's job had relocated us into a large apartment while we looked for a house. We went from a very spacious home to an apartment that was large, but was only half the size of what we were used to. I believe that this was God's plan yet again.

During this time of living in a smaller place, our family grew very close. For the first time we knew that our son and daughter would be joining our other two children in day to day activities with us, and we were eager to spend this time with them. God used this time to strengthen our family as we learned to live together again. Eventually, we moved on to a much larger home, but our time together in that apartment was unforgettable.

Jerry and I were also excited to return to our home town and begin attending our home church. We had been working with our Pastor to launch a new NAME Center and train couples in the church to be Certified Marriage Specialists who would offer marriage and pre-marriage counseling to couples. It was our heart's desire to continue to help other couples by strengthening and empowering their marriage and family. We were able to plant this new marriage counseling center in our home church with seven couples available to provide crisis counseling at no cost.

As I said earlier, happily ever after is what you make of it, and our happily ever after continued to bring challenges. While we were still praising God for the victory in the court, we were reminded of what it means to be a blended family. When people divorce, they sometimes assume that they will be divorcing all of their problems. They fail to realize that divorce not only keeps most of your problems, but it adds thousands of new ones, especially if you have children.

Not long after the verdict in Jerry's custody case was received and his case was at an end in Oklahoma, my own custody case began. This was the first time since the original divorce that I was facing a modification to the custody of my two boys.

Jerry's case was moved to Missouri and this provided an opportunity for changes in that custody matter. Once again, we were forced to shell out thousands of dollars to keep our family together after another custody modification was filed. Now we were faced with not one, but two court cases. That brings double the stress, double the financial strain, and double the time wasted.

We knew that God would keep our family together, and we once again put all of our trust in His divine plan. We had received the promise, and God was not about to take it away.

We were by no means happy about the situation, yet we still walked in joy and peace throughout the entire process. We often tell others that when it comes to working with your ex-spouse you must always do the right thing, even when your feelings don't match up and you do not want to. In some cases you need to weigh the cost of the court battle against what you are fighting for.

Jerry and I both offered to come to an agreement that would keep us from spending more time and money in court. We agreed to give them more visitation out of mercy. We knew that the children were growing up quickly and it wouldn't be long before they would be off to college, and it allowed them to spend more time with their other parents.

In our case, we didn't want our ex-spouses to continue the pain and anxiety that we had experienced while we navigated the court system. We did not want to contaminate our testimony of how God had made a promise, walked with us through the pain and suffering, and brought us through stronger and victorious.

We wanted to be gracious and merciful, and give more to our ex-spouses than they may have given us in the same situation. I pray that in some way this small gesture will glorify God, and bring them both closer to Him.

At the time of this writing, it has been about four years since our miraculous victory in the court and since we brought our two children home just as God had promised. Our son is still recovering from his growth deficit, but he is catching up. For the first time since early childhood he is on the growth chart for height and weight. He still has a long way to go, and it is more apparent when you stand him next to our other son who is eleven months older. Our son should be closer to his height, but we believe that God is doing another miracle by growing his body, and he will fully recover someday soon.

God has already healed him of many of the issues that had once gripped him. He is no longer the anxious, worried little boy that he was. He is a strong, caring, compassionate young man. His amazing love for other people and his willingness to serve is inspiring to me.

Just the other day I was brought to tears when he reminded me of how he used to stand on the bed and measure how tall God would make him against my own height. Now he is almost taller than I am! I pray with him and we ask that God will make him grow to well over six feet tall so that he will have an amazing testimony of the walking miracle that he is.

Our daughter is a beautiful, brilliant teenager who works very hard to make the most of her blended family situation. I know that it is still a struggle for her to be torn between the events at her mother's house and the events here with us, but we strive to make it uncomplicated for her. She and I are great friends and we enjoy getting away from our house full of guys to have girl time together.

She recently blessed me with an amazing note of gratitude for the time I spend parenting her. It touched my spirit to know that she could recognize the mother's heart that I have for her and to appreciate it. She is going to make a great wife someday!

Our oldest son is finishing up his freshman year of college at an engineering university where he dreams of using his intellect to serve God through science. He has felt called by God to work in engineering for biomedical sciences that may result in restoring muscle movements to people with spinal cord injuries. We are so thankful for how he still allows God to guide his steps, and we look forward to what God will accomplish through him.

Our other son is looking forward to his senior year of high school and dreams of becoming a doctor.

We are very proud of how well he stands up for his faith in Christ in his public school. He uses his life verse of 1 Corinthians 6:9-10 to explain why he does not agree with certain lifestyle choices of some of his friends. He hopes that he can be a light in the darkness that some of the other students find themselves in.

Jerry and I now find ourselves raising a fifth child, one who we will be adopting in just a few months. We've added a new kind of blended to our family by adopting from the foster care system. It has furthered our knowledge and our sadness to discover that there are so many children caught in the middle of their parents' poor choices. Our daughter has a story of her own, yet now she can finally heal and learn what it means to be a part of a family who takes care of her, encourages her, and most of all loves her.

We remain steadfast in the mission to make a difference by devoting our time and energy in marriage ministry. Marriage ministry begins with one person striving to become a healthy and whole individual. They must deepen their relationship with God, and learn to lean on Him with people of this world fail them. Then, and only then, can these two people marry and successfully weather the storms that life will bring.

Forsaken

My God, my God, why have you forsaken me? Why are you so far from saving me, so far from my cries of anguish?

~ Psalm 22:1

About three in the afternoon Jesus cried out in a loud voice, "Eli, Eli, lema sabachthani?" (which means 'My God, my God, why have you forsaken me?')

~ Matthew 27:46

For we do not have a high priest who is unable to empathize with our weaknesses, but we have one who has been tempted in every way, just as we are—yet he did not sin.

~ Hebrews 4:15

    After going through all we had gone through over the years, seeing these verses side by side makes the words come alive. In the first verse, David is calling out to God questioning why he was being forsaken. He felt abandoned and alone, a feeling that we have all felt at some time or another.

    In the second verse, not only was that verse uttered at the moment just before the mysterious miracle of salvation was about to take place, it illustrates that we have a Savior who can relate to us. I believe this verse shows us God really does know our pain. He knows our desire to be known. He knows what it feels like to feel forsaken, because He actually was forsaken.

    This verse is certainly not a contradiction, but a reminder of Christ's empathy for us, especially when you follow it up with that third verse listed in this chapter. A great example of the point of this is summed up in the shortest verse in the Bible, John 11:35 *"Jesus wept."*

    He wept before He raised Lazarus from the dead, because He loved His friends and understood the grief they were going through. Jesus knew He was going to raise Lazarus even before He created the earth, yet He still wept tears of compassion and empathized with His friends.

    What I learned was that despite my feelings of desperation and loneliness, the truth was that I was never really forsaken. My God was empathizing with me in my pain and in my weakness. His power was being made perfect in that weakness, but there were times when I couldn't see past my circumstances to even notice.

Maybe I began with a circumstantial faith, but over time it has grown into so much more. My faith is no longer dependent on my circumstances. We could have allowed our pain to turn into the poison of unforgiveness. Instead, with God's help we turned that pain into passion. We now have a passion to help and encourage others who are hurting.

Jesus said we will have trials in this life because we lived in a fallen world. He also said those trials wouldn't last forever. Nor would they be a waste, because He has a greater purpose.

Through our trials He develops our character and builds our faith. He is preparing us for His purpose and for Heaven. When trials come, we need to trust God's purpose in our pain. We may not always see that purpose, but if we take the time to look we can see His hand in our circumstances.

We should never waste the opportunity available in a trial. I think that is what the author of James 2 was talking about when he said to consider it pure joy to suffer for the cause of Christ. He also says our trials test our faith and produces perseverance. He knew the work of perseverance would finish the work of perfection in each of us so that we lack nothing.

All those years it felt like we were in the middle of relentless fire. Sometimes it felt like our continuous testing had no end in sight. It was years of constant exhaustion for us.

We held fast to His promises that we would be vindicated by the truth. We may have had every reason to be angry and not forgive, but we do not have a right to withhold forgiveness of others if we want to participate in the forgiveness of our own sins.

When He became sin for us who had sinned, He felt the sting of death and the failure we all feel when we sin. He was perfect, yet, He humbled Himself for us. When He cried out to the Father in anguish about his feelings of being forsaken, He demonstrated that He can relate to us.

Nobody knows me better than my Father in Heaven, and now I know that He loves me. Because of what Christ did on the cross for me and for all of us, He has shown me what it really is to be forsaken. I know now that He is telling the truth when He says that He will never leave me nor forsake me.

Show me your ways, LORD, teach me your paths. Guide me in your truth and teach me, for you are God my Savior, and my hope is in you all day long.

~ Psalm 25:4-5

It's no accident that you're reading this book. You, too, may have walked through fire. Maybe you're even walking through fire right now. Perhaps you are struggling to see any anything beyond your current situation, let alone God's plan for your life. Perhaps you're struggling with your past, as I did. Maybe you're having trouble forgiving those who hurt you. Maybe you doubt yourself because of past mistakes. I can relate.

In my past I was abandoned, abused, neglected, hurt, and seemingly forsaken. I used my past circumstances to label myself. Then I let that label hinder me from doing what God had called me to do.

The more I read the Bible, the more I realized that God has always used flawed people in mighty ways. He has even used people who had done far worse things than I had ever done. As I continued to read God's word, I am continually surprised at how God called his people to do big things. He actually called them to do huge things for His purposes, and He also used them to perform tremendous miracles.

In fact, God seemed to pluck David right out of a regular, ordinary family and turned him into a King. David was the eighth son, which meant that he would likely have only a tiny inheritance. His brothers would be far richer than he would be, and thus he became content as a shepherd. God anointed David and gave him a clear word about how he would be King one day. Even though David used his power as king to commit adultery and murder, God allowed him to remain on the throne. In fact He said this of David, "...God testified concerning him: 'I have found David son of Jesse, a man after my own heart;" (Acts 13:22) even knowing what he would later do.

Joseph was also one of the youngest sons in a large family. He was loved by his father, but he was still abused, abandoned, and even sold into slavery in Potiphar's house by his jealous brothers. Just as Joseph was beginning to recover from his brothers' betrayal in Potiphar's house, he was falsely accused of rape and imprisoned for about fourteen years. Yet, God raised him up to become the second most powerful ruler in all of Egypt and the world; just as God showed Joseph through his dreams as He had promised.

Out of fear for himself, Abraham lied to the Egyptian ruler about his wife. His lie caused her to be abducted and added to the Pharaoh's harem. Even after God delivered them from that debacle, Sarah doubted God's promise to give her and Abraham a son. When it didn't happen as quickly as she wanted, she took matters into her own hands. She nagged Abraham so severely; he finally caved to her demand to have a child through her slave, Hagar. Their actions have wreaked havoc on every generation throughout the world ever since. Still, God fulfilled His promise to both of them and Isaac was born.

Clearly, your story and my story are not unique. Time and again I hear stories of people who have endured far more pain and suffering than me. Women and children worldwide are being forced into sexual slavery every day. Families are being torn apart by the violence in their homes or the tragedies of war. Christians are being martyred for their faith in front of the whole world. People are suffering and dying from incurable diseases. Children are abused, neglected, and abandoned by their own parents.

Lately, the news is filled with reports of bacteria, viruses, and plagues far worse than cancer, HIV, and AIDS. Earthquakes, tsunami's, floods, hurricanes, tornadoes, and other natural disasters destroy lives by the masses. Entire nations are under the control of terrorists, or living in fear of a terrorist attack.

Men and women are being falsely imprisoned. Many are losing their families in the process. Thousands of people are living with a permanent mark on their lives from mistakes they have made in the past. Marks such as "sex offender, murderer, drunk driver, rapist, or swindler." Even if they repent, change their entire life, change their perspective, and pay a debt to society, they may never recover from the effects of their actions over the course of their lifetime.

In fact, somewhere in this huge world, at this very moment, someone is suffering far more than you and I ever will.

Yet, we must not allow our circumstances to dictate our emotions. We can choose to be blessed, even when everything is coming against us. We can choose joy when we would rather feel destitute. We can choose to trust God and believe He is in control, rather than trying to control people and situations through our own power. We can choose to allow God to use our testimony to tell the story of His love, mercy, grace, and glory.

No, it isn't an accident that you're reading this book; because, God wants to use you in a mighty way. Whether you are starting from ground zero as I did, or you're a seasoned Christian, God has something amazing in store for your life.

If you will press into God, like a child presses into their father for comfort and support; if you will spend time in God's Word and in prayer you will hear Him speak to you. The promises He makes will come to pass. You need only be patient and trust in God's perfect timing, not yours!

You might be questioning what possible good can come from your situation. You might even feel God has abandoned you in this time of great need. But, take comfort in knowing that you and I have a High Priest who empathizes with the pain you are experiencing. This pain is because of sin.

Sin may not have been part of God's original plan for us, but in His mercy He has created a way to free us from it's grip. More importantly, part of His divine plan for our lives is to give us a way of escape.

If you are reading this book and you are like I was, never truly knowing Jesus as our savior and not understanding His unconditional love, then I urge you to take the first step in ultimate healing. Surrender your life to Jesus and ask Him to forgive you of your sins. Declare that He is Lord, and that you desire to fully know His plan for your life.

When you accept His plan of salvation, and start to search out the meaning behind everything you have encountered, you may find yourself still struggling to know the peace and joy that I've talked about. Don't worry; this is normal. We are after all, only human. Our pain is real and we really feel it. Find a Bible based church that will disciple you. That is, one that will teach you about God, Jesus, and the Bible. Find other Godly people to mentor you, and make heart connections with them by sharing your struggles.

Just because you have made the decision to follow Jesus does not mean that all of your suffering will end. If anything, this book has given you a representation of my own trials even after I surrendered everything to God. When I questioned these trials, my mentor said that the enemy doesn't battle on ground he has already won. This means that the enemy will fight to discourage us, and to keep us from sharing the gospel with others.

Even though we all still face the trials of life, we can cling to something that is more powerful than the enemy. We are not alone in the battle. We not only have other Christians to battle side by side with us, but we have Jesus. We can cling to Jesus and His grace, His mercy, and His unending, unconditional love. When we accept salvation, and we trust God's plan for our lives, then we can experience healing, joy. Best of all, we will never, ever, have to feel forsaken!

http://marriageawakening.com

www.ingramcontent.com/pod-product-compliance
Lightning Source LLC
Chambersburg PA
CBHW070735020526
44118CB00035B/1367